World War I Genealogy Research Guide

Tracing American Military
and Non-Combatant Ancestors
Includes a Guide to Canadian Military Research

By Debra M. Dudek

Copyright © 2018 by Debra M. Dudek

All rights reserved. No part of this publication may be reproduced, distributed, or transmitted in any form or by any means, including photocopying, recording, or other electronic or mechanical methods, without the prior written permission of the publisher, except in the case of brief quotations embodied in critical reviews and certain other noncommercial uses permitted by copyright law. For permission requests, e-mail the author with the subject "Attention: Permissions Requested," at debradudek@yahoo.com.

First Edition

To Tina and Jeff

'Thank You' is too common a phrase

Table of Contents

Introduction By the Author	3
Before You Begin Your Research	7
Research Goals	11
WWI Research Online: United States	17
State Specific Collections and Resources	41
Examining Essential Records at the National Archives	55
Naturalization and Enemy Alien Records	67
Non-Military Women's World War I Records	77
Short Guide Guide to Canadian World War I	87

Introduction By the Author

The First World War is one of America's forgotten conflicts. Even during the centennial year of America's entry into the war in April 2017, it barely registered as a blip in the public consciousness. Ask a few random people in the street, and the response is generally the same. There was a First World War, because we had a second one. As to the specifics, not much is known. Occasionally, I'll meet someone who's grandfather or great-grandfather served in the war. Another relative, like a parent or the grandparent has all the memorabilia. Medals, and uniforms, and pictures. There's pride there, but the connection to the person or the war itself, is very vague. Ask about the Second World War, and there's more conversation. More specifics. Movies, books, documentaries. Grandparents or great-uncles who told them about serving in Europe or in the South Pacific.

While the Great War is lesser known of the two world wars, the former tends to be lumped in with the latter. The events of both wars are present when historians, writers, lecturers, and genealogists highlight America's rise to power in the 20th century.

As a researcher and lecturer, I see the same issues among the genealogical community when the topic of the Great War pops up. Yes, there are people who know or suspect their ancestor served, but the barriers to American research seem like an unrewarding struggle with limited return on investment. And this lack of motivation is unusual amongst weekend and even dedicated genealogists. This lack of enthusiasm is strange, as genealogists by and large are a group of people who will spend hours shifting through tax rolls for three separate counties in a succession of creepy basements and ill lit storage rooms just to pinpoint an ancestor's migration year from one state to the next. This same group could potentially spend years attending lectures and searching for copies of 'burned' courthouse records with a song in their heart. Entire genealogical careers are built on locating copies of 'burned records' from courthouses and churches to city and municipal government archives.

I don't blame genealogists in general for this oversight, but I do attribute one loaded statement for from the US National Archives system for the lack of optimism in Great War research:

On July 12, 1973, a disastrous fire at the National Personnel Records Center (NPRC) destroyed approximately 16-18 million Official Military Personnel Files (OMPF). The records affected:

Branch	Personnel and Period Affected	Estimated Loss
Army	Discharges November 1, 1912 to January 1, 1960	80%
Air Force	Discharges September 25, 1947 to January 1, 1964	75%

(with names alphabetically after Hubbard, James E.)

Approximately 16-18 million Army Official Military Personnel Files from the Great War, including the records from the Army Air Service, were damaged or destroyed in the 1973 fire. A large portion of World War II Army, Army Air Corps, and Air Force records as well, and modern researchers are cranking out books left and right about those subjects.

You know what other country lost a bulk of their WWI records in a fire? Great Britain. That's right. Good old Blighty lost upward of 60% of their Great War service files during the London Blitz, and they're pumping out so many books, movies, and documentaries about the Great War that the conflict generates cultural attention and recognition from around the world. Remember the Great War years featured in *Downton Abbey*, and the critically acclaimed movie and stage production of *War Horse*? How about the comedic genius of *Blackadder Goes Forth*? Not to mention the barrage of other BBC movies and miniseries featuring characters from or in the Great War?

Great Britain has made up for their loss of service records by working with the British Library, their National Archives, and partnering with genealogy websites like FindMyPast, Ancestry, and Fold3, to make as many different record sets as possible available to researchers. Records such as World War I pension records, hospital registers, prisoner of war lists, wounded and missing servicemen reports, servicewomen casualty lists, court martials, military desertions, daily war diaries, and other highly detailed collections are available to genealogists and historians. A true majority of these records are fully searchable and available online, even if you may have to pay to view them if you're accessing them from the National Archives site directly.

When encountering a brick wall, burned courthouse, or natural disaster where a set of records are almost completely wiped off the face of the earth, the next step for a genealogist is to look at what records ARE available, and how they can be used toward accomplishing an end goal. Anyone who is familiar with researching burned church and courthouse records, or anyone collecting documents of their Irish ancestry will know full well how to scrape and chase after all sorts of digital and offline records to find an accurate birth date, event location, or maiden name to add to the family tree.

The 'records burned' mantra should have been an opportunity to expound and highlight the types of records which are readily available and start releasing indexes and digitizing record sets as in the years leading up to the centennial. Funding, lack of public attention, and the financial crisis in the United States ensured this cultural explosion of records never really had a chance to happen.

In the four years I spent researching *Someplace Not Far from Terror* as well as this research guide, my Great War topic began to feel like the middle child at the dinner table – constantly overlooked and misunderstood by others. Thankfully, I'm a middle child, so I'd adjusted well enough to simply smile and nod politely when others fumbled to come up with a response in kind, or to ignore the grimaces on the faces of the people who were charged with gathering my records.

My one relief was researching in Ottawa, where I had an absolutely outstanding experience sorting through records at the Canadian War Museum and the Library and Archives of Canada. Great War research isn't considered an anomaly in Canada, and for that fact, I'm truly grateful.

It is my hope as you progress with your research, the information you find will help bring to light the experience of your Great War ancestors. What you choose to document and research today paves the way for success for the genealogists following you. We've probably all had help documenting and discovering our ancestry with the help of a hardworking genealogist somewhere in the past. Don't just give future generations the World War I equivalent of a message in a bottle. Give them a whole damn library.

Good Luck with Your Search!

Before You Begin

When I started researching the military aspects of World War I generation, I had no idea where to go, where to start, or what kind of records would be available. I had absolutely nothing. No photographs. No letters. No discharge papers. Nothing. The small pocket diary in my family's possession belonged to an entirely different man. Due to a house fire in 1932, any documentation or military service details and photographs of my ancestor were destroyed. I also lived several hours away from county or state record depositories where information may have been housed. Interviewing relatives also proved to be a complete bust. No one had unit or personal details apart from two phrases.

"Grandpa Rhodes was an ambulance driver in France during the First World War. He never talked about it."

No one at that time had published a genealogy 'quick guide' to World War I research. I stumbled around for a few years, feeling as if I was the clumsiest genealogist on the planet. However, with time, tenacity, and a willingness to travel, I was able to collect the information I needed to recreate my ancestor's Great War experience. I was also exceptionally lucky, as my great-grandfather's official World War I military service file survived the Personnel Records Center fire almost completely intact. The forty-some page file arrived by mail in all its photo copied glory, the edges of each paper charred extra crispy.

Before I even thought I'd be fortunate to own a service file, I was poking around at state depositories, keeping notes on record keeping standards for the time period, as well as e-mailing and calling every relative in my grandmother's contact book searching for alternative ways to find information. Those efforts paid off more than I ever anticipated.

The goal of this guide is to give you a straight forward approach to your research; to help you discover the specifics of your ancestor's great war service, whether they served at home or abroad, and how to complete your goal using a mixture of online and physical resources. Even starting with nothing but a family story is a step forward on the path to acquiring a better understanding of your ancestor's World War I experience. Completing a successful research project in this field is more attainable now than it was just a few years ago.

What Makes the Great War Great for Genealogists?
The Great War transitioned an old world into a new modern era. Through an explosion in exports, it gave America the opportunity to become a major player on the world stage. The Great War influenced rapid change at home and abroad, and nowhere is this more telling than in its paper trail. In many of the microfilmed and physical papers created during the war, most of them are either a combination of printed documents with handwriting or are made up of entirely typeset items. In the three biggest resources everyone should have access to, all the records are completely typed, easy to read and popping crisply off the page. Even the carbon copies look great.

Americans had a unique contribution to the Great War
Although the country entered the war at a much later date, they were able to reinforce Allied battle lines and distinguish themselves both on and off the battlefield. With a fresh supply of troops, the Americans also brought with them the massive muscle power of large motor trucks and touring cars alleviating the need for animal power. The Quartermaster Corps and the Amy Corps of Engineers were in charge of building and transporting the logistical lines of travel for the Allied forces, and the Signal Corps captured thousands of photographs both in the sky and on land.

There May be a Reason Why Your Ancestor Was Mum About Their Service
It's easy to say 'War is Hell', and assume every American had the same

experience while they served in uniform at home and abroad. The Great War itself is such an intricate and many faceted series of events, that it's easy to get lost in the iconic images instead of the realities each person faced. Men who enlisted as bakers, coffee rosters, waggoneers, and chauffeurs, railroad men, engineers, and mechanics are not often praised for their service. Women who served as nurses, yeomen, chauffeurs, telephone operators and in clerical positions were until quite recently, rarely celebrated for their contributions. Who knows? Your ancestor could have served or volunteered with Walt Disney, Amelia Earhart, E.E. Cummings, and the other writers, poets, and artists of the lost generation. A brush of greatness which sometimes occurs during wartime.

With service comes sacrifice. The bombardments, poison gas, disease, and grind of warfare took its tole on men and women, military personnel and civilians alike. The horrors of war were not reserved solely for front line troops. Soldiers assigned to support roles such as identifying and interring remains, as well as rebuilding bridges and railroads witnessed death at first hand. The war played a role in the psychological health as well as the physical health of veterans and volunteers after the war.

Research Online vs. Archive and Library Research
No one can deny how the availability of genealogy and history resources has exploded in the last decade. Taking technology into consideration, you will want to look at your research checklist and search through online and traditional brick and mortar resources. In your quest for online records, do not underestimate sites such as Internet Archive or your state and local historical organizations.

An Important Note on Women's Records
Women's records will vary depending on their wartime role. While thousands of women moved into careers and provided much needed services during the Great War, their contributions have been until quite recently, under appreciated. Nurses who enlisted and served within the US military, such as the Army, Marine, and Navy Corps, will have military service records.

Due to the NPRC fire in 1973, the service files of the Army Nursing Corps had suffered damage and loss on the same scale quoted by the

National Archives. Similarly, to the WWI records of the Marines and Navy, the nursing corps records for these two branches have survived intact to the present day.

Women also had an opportunity to serve as Navy Yeomen in the US Naval Reserves, and their records are complete and highly detailed.

There were several positions available to women in the US Army Signal Corps such as clerks, office workers, and telephone operators. Although they were sworn in and received government training, uniforms, and adhered to military regulations, the women serving in these positions were considered civilians and did not receive honorable discharges at the end of the war. As civilians, they were considered to be more akin to contractors than enlisted individuals.

Be on the lookout for female ancestors who served in volunteer organizations such as the Women's Committee and the American Red Cross. Women were a driving force for raising liberty bonds, hosting fundraisers, and volunteering their time at hospitals and service agencies throughout the country. Women were also involved with domestic investigation organizations such as the American Protective League, American Defense League, and other groups who assisted in documenting subversion and illegal acts for the Federal Bureau of Investigation during the Great War.

Chapter 1 - Research Goals & an Introduction to Online Research

The important first step in beginning a new genealogical project is to establish goals and outline a research plan. Every individual may have their own idea of what information they wish to acquire during their research, and with that in mind, this chapter will provide examples of research goals, and provide a research checklist to begin your project.

Goal #1 - Find out if your ancestor served

You may have a family story, an odd assortment of photographs, or found a line in an obituary which led you on the hunt of a WWI military ancestor. There may be other smaller details which have popped up in the course of your research, such as a US BIRLS death file or a military issued headstone which has caused you to scratch your head and ask more questions.

When beginning your journey, take time to look through your family's collection of items, and network with other relatives to find and obtain the following resources.

- WWI Draft Registration Cards
- Obituary Notices
- Photographs
- Military Discharge Papers
- Veterans Administration Paperwork
- Old Postcards and Letters
- Family Stories (Write what you know and record other relatives)

- Details of Service from Veterans Groups – American Legion, Veterans of Foreign Wars, Marine Corps League, Military Order of the Cootie
- Newspaper clippings
- Oral Histories

Goal #2 - Find your Veteran's Rank and Unit Information

At first glance, this can appear to be tricky. There are thankfully, both official and collateral resources you can use to help collect this data. The National Personnel Records Center and the National Archives in St. Louis may not have what you want online presently, however, there are several records which are readily available by online request with payment or free to collect on microfilm during an in-person visit. Details of placing an online records request for full service records and final payment vouchers are available online at https://www.archives.gov/veterans/military-service-records.

If you are planning to make a trip in person, it is necessary to make an appointment to visit the archives. Plan ahead of your trip to secure an appointment date. The average wait time for a response to a research visit request can range from several weeks to two months. There is no appointment needed to view records (like muster rolls) which are available on microfilm. During your visit, you may scan and photograph records free of charge (with some restrictions). Photo copies can be requested for an additional fee of $.75 per page.

Here are some of the best records to begin your research:

- Official Military Personnel Files & Final Payment Voucher Rolls (Navy, Marines, and some Army and Air Force items)
- Final Payment Voucher
- Unit Muster Rolls

In addition to federal records you can request from the National Personnel Records Center and the National Archives, you can begin an online research strategy. Not all the resources you need for your project will be online, but you can definitely start your search with the following websites:

- Ancestry.com
- Chronicling America
- FamilySearch
- Fold3
- Google Books
- Google News Archive
- Hathi Trust
- Internet Archive
- Paid newspaper subscription sites
- State Newspaper Collections
- State World War I Collections

If your ancestor was enlisted in the Navy, Coast Guard, or Marine Corps, these items were not affected by the National Archives fire disaster. Sending away for these files should be a swift and straight forward process. Army and National Guard record availability can vary by individual. Remember, the US Air Force was not established until 1947. If you are researching pilots, they were part of the US Army Air Service, and later in the Army Air Corps until 1947. These records will be found under Army files, which a large portion were damaged or destroyed in the NPRC fire.

If you have already sent away for final payment voucher or military service record online from the National Personnel Records Center, you don't have to twiddle your thumbs waiting for a response. Some resources, such as state veterans bonus registrations, county histories, discharge papers, may be available online, so see what's available to you by location. Don't rule out non-digitized collections. Remember, you can always call upon other helpful genealogists on Facebook research groups or a veteran's service group who may be able to pick up essential items for you on your behalf. Also, libraries, archives, genealogical societies, and historical societies, can send items to you by e-mail for free or at a low cost.

Goal #3 - Find dates of service, as well as details of service
Using a combination of military service files, newspaper accounts, and

veteran's bonus records, you should be able to begin piecing together a time line of your ancestor's service. Should you receive little to no information from the NPRC regarding dates of service, do not fret! There are some amazing online and microfilm resources which can help you reconstruct a service time line without the use of a full military service file.

Here are a few resources which will help you achieve this goal:
- Unit Histories (Personal and official publications)
- County Honor Roll Books
- Headstone Applications and Veteran's Administration Records Online
- Army and Coast Guard Muster Rolls on Microfilm at the National Archives
- Official Camp and Unit Newsletters and Newspapers
- Newspaper Articles
- Museum and Archive Collections
- Private Diaries and Correspondence

Goal #4 – Brush Up On World War I History & Geography

The Great War is such a big subject, it is easy to look at the scope of the conflict and feel completely lost. You do not need to be a history expert or attempt to take on an epic quest to understand every event which happened. Start small. Begin with your ancestor. Where were they living in 1917 before war was declared? Take your ancestor's dates of service and plug them in on a time line. The beauty of those WWI muster rolls is how they account for your ancestor's location at the end of each month. Just like a federal census record, you know exactly where they are at the end of each month. Now, throw in some unit histories along with some of the location names you've found from your collateral records on to your time line. You can also use these resources for additional time line reference points.

- County Histories of the Great War (or World War) published in the early 1920s
- County Honor Rolls published in the 1920s
- Unit Histories and Published Memoirs
- Interactive WWI Timeline (https://www.theworldwar.org/

explore/interactive-wwi-timeline)
- WW1 Timeline — a Detailed Timeline of the Great War (http://www.greatwar.co.uk/timeline/ww1-timeline.htm)
- First World War On This Day Calendar (http://www.firstworldwar.com/onthisday/january.htm)
- The Great War Video Series (https://www.youtube.com/user/TheGreatWar)
- Crash Course US and World History (https://www.youtube.com/user/crashcourse)

Goal #5 – Find Service Details in Veteran's Post-War Life

Veteran's groups such as the American Legion organized and advocated to expand services and resources for soldiers and sailors promptly after the end of World War I. Having forged friendships and connections during military service, the American Legion organized social events, published a newsletter, lobbied for World War I Adjusted Compensation Act (veterans bonus), and pushed for better employment opportunities for veterans returning home from service, as well as expanding disability payments to affected individuals. The American Legion also shone a light on the need for establishing a hospital system for veterans, as there were no facilities for treating reoccurring and psychological injuries specifically for men who had served in Europe. Lectures detailing military benefits also were particularly popular.

Finding your ancestor in the adjusted compensation 'bonus register' is a particular treat, as it may have provided the down payment for a home they owned in the 1930 census or made it possible to purchase their first automobile. Reexamine any family stories about a home or big-ticket item purchase in 1924 or 1925.

As a genealogist, you have the ability to shape and share your family's narrative. All the items you've collected and documented can help future generations with their own research. Your accomplishments and ability share what you know today will help future researchers, writers, educators, and students understand the events of a century ago, so don't forget to cite your sources!

Goal #6 – Share Your Veteran's World War I Story

With a majority of your research completed, it's time to share your ancestor's service with the wider world. Using the World War I centennial as a springboard, you may wish to share the results of your research by:

- Writing a short description of your ancestor's service and share it online as a PDF document among family and friends
- Writing about the research process and your findings for a local newspaper, genealogical or historical society newsletter
- Presenting your findings as a narrative with pictures at your local genealogical society, veteran's post, Daughters of the American Revolution or Sons of the American Revolution meeting
- Submitting a small summary of your research to the local historical society or museum where your ancestor lived or enlisted. Include copies of photographs.
- Recording the story of ancestor's service as a video or audio session.
- Sharing what you learned in a blog or social media post online
- Making a donation to the World War I Memorial in Washington DC or the National World War I Museum and Memorial in Kansas City, along with a summary of your ancestor's service

Enclosed in this book, you will find a full research list which will help keep you on track as you begin compiling information on your World War I ancestor. There is also a free downloadable research list available on my website. This list can be filled out as you move forward through the research process and provides places to search and records to examine which should build your soldier's service profile. To help you check off the items on your research list, this next section will provide examples of resources and what information they contain. This is by no means a list of every single resource available. Remember, take a look at what you can find on a local, state, and regional level to help supplement federal resources.

Chapter 2 - WWI Research Online: United States

The online aspect of World War I genealogy research doesn't seem like a straightforward proposition. To help you cut through the noise of a general genealogy search, you will want to focus your initial efforts to searching collections which will yield the best return on your efforts. There is no such thing as 'one stop' research area for American World War I records.

This chapter will help you form a workable research strategy online. These resources will lead you to records and items which should assist in tracking down the information you need from the comfort of your home computer. These sources will help lead you to additional items found in physical depositories and a variety of archives.

Ancestry.com
The three major sources for American World War One records on Ancestry.com provide the first building blocks to your genealogy research. These resources should be the first in a multi-part plan for hunting down facts and information. All three of these record sets are not listed under the World War I Military topic area of Ancestry.com, which is why you may not have used them before.

U.S., Department of Veterans Affairs BIRLS Death File, 1850-2010
The US Beneficiary Identification Records Locater Subsystem provides birth, death, and enlistment information for more than 14 million veterans and VA beneficiaries who died between the years 1850 and 2010. This is of particular importance for World War I veterans, as it provides solid military enlistment and release dates to add to your

research.

Examine records and add this information to your checklist:
- Birth Date
- Death Date
- Enlistment Date
- Release Date

U.S., Army Transport Service, Passenger Lists, 1910-1939

Contained within an intact World War I military service file is a single sheet of paper which records all the vital transport information for a journey across the ocean to Europe. To have access to the original record at the National Archives, a researcher would have needed to have an account of the date and ship name to find a specific veterans name. It was a boon to genealogists when the National Archives partnered with Ancestry to digitize these records.

These troop passenger lists document the movement of American military personnel and ships going to and from Europe during WWI, and beyond. The records include details that might not be accessible or available to researchers.
- Name of Veteran
- Rank and Service Unit
- Military Serial Service Number
- Departure Date and Place
- Next of Kin and Relationship
- Notes

Examine records and add this information to your checklist:
- Rank
- Military Unit Information
- Service Number
- Next of Kin Information

Transport lists are for soldiers who are being moved to and from Europe, so domestic travel is not recorded in this record set. As with every journey, theres travel to and from a destination, so you will find a departure listing and a return listing. Even if a soldier had died during service, his family had the option to repatriate remains back to the United States. Transportation listings include shipping and information for the remains of soldiers being moved back to a cemetery in America.

Tip: Include the address (street, city, state) for a soldiers next of kin in your search. It will help differentiate between individuals with the same name in your query results.

The departure and return listings may provide a contrast or updated unit information.

U.S., Headstone Applications for Military Veterans, 1925-1963
This database contains application forms for headstones for deceased members and veterans of the U.S. armed services. Applications were made between 1925 and 1963. Forms vary by date.

Examine Records and add this information to your checklist:
- Name
- Serial Number
- Pension Number
- Enlistment Date
- Discharge Date
- Service
- Date of birth and death
- Headstone order date
- Name, Address, Signature, of applicant
- Name and Location of Cemetery
- Office Notes & Signatures

Add to Checklist or Double Check:
- Serial Number
- Pension Number
- Enlistment and Discharge Date
- Inconsistencies or Differences in Service Details
- Date of Birth and Date of Death
- Location of Remains
- Name of Cemetery

* * *

The World War I page on Ancestry may look a little sparse in caparison to the resources listed for other topics, such as the Revolutionary War, Civil War, and World War II. While the following list is by no means reflects the entire bulk of Great War records on the site, the record sets below will give you develop a to-do list of sets to search.

Navy & Marine Specific
- *U.S., Navy and Marine Corps Registries, 1814-1992*
- *U.S. Marine Corps Muster Rolls, 1798-1958*
- *U.S. Navy Support Books, 1901-1902, 1917-2010*
- *U.S. Navy Cruise Books, 1918-2009*
- *U.S., World War I Naval Deaths, 1917-1919*

General
- *U.S., Lists of Men Ordered to Report to Local Board for Military Duty, 1917-1918*
- *U.S., World War I Soldier Naturalizations, 1918*
- *Kansas, Camp Funston Military Records, 1914-1919*
- *Kansas, World War I Veteran Collection, 1917-1919*
- *U.S. National Homes for Disabled Volunteer Soldiers, 1866-1938*
- *U.S., World War I Draft Registration Cards, 1917-1918*
- *WWI, WWII, and Korean War Casualty Listings*
- *U.S. Veterans' Gravesites, ca.1775-2006*

State Specific Records on Ancestry
- *California, World War I Death Announcements, 1918-1921*
- *Connecticut, Military Census, 1917*
- *Maryland Military Men, 1917-1918*
- *New Mexico, World War I Records, 1917-1919*
- *New York, Abstracts of World War I Military Service, 1917-1919*
- *New York, Military Service Cards, 1816-1979*
- *New York, World War I Veterans' Service Data, 1913-1919*
- *Ohio Soldiers in WWI, 1917-1918*
- *Utah, Military Records, 1861-1970 - WWI Service Questionnaires*
- *Utah, Veterans with Federal Service Buried in Utah,1847-1966*

Nursing Files

- *U.S., American Red Cross Nurse Files, 1916-1959*

FamilySearch
You may not equate FamilySearch.org as a place for World War I military records or service files. However, their large scale efforts to digitize microfilm which began in late 2017 is already making an impact on the availability of not only WWI military discharge records, but of compiled military service files, and veterans bonus records as well.

To find WWI military service records on FamilySearch, you will need to do a little digging. There is a new category in the search area of the site. After selecting a country and state/province, resist the urge to use the search box or Search Historical Records area at the top of the page. Instead, scroll down to the Image-Only Historical Records and Catalog Material area. The image only collection is full of items which havent been indexed yet, while the catalog items are brimming with new digitized records which have been transferred from the FamilySearch microfilm collection. There are several ways to browse by topic.

The Catalog collection can be narrowed down by topic by using the drop-down box at the top of the section. All the new digitized items which havent made their way to the searchable or browsable collections are being stored here, so there are a ton of different options. When performing a search for Michigan World War I records, I looked under the Catalog Material section and selected the Military collection in the drop down box. There are over 700 items available, and most of them were from the Civil War. Selecting the Show All link, there are clickable options to narrow results down by time period, however, you may not find these particularly helpful. Remember, the scope of Civil War records extend well beyond the dates of the actual war, and are spread out among headstone applications, pension indexes, Grand Army of the Republic rosters, and records of service.

At the time of publication, military records on FamilySearch are not separated by war or conflict. This feature may be added as the site continues to add new record sets of digitized records. If this scrolling through hundreds of newly digitized military files proves to be a bit overwhelming, focus your efforts on the FamilySearch catalog area of their website - https://www.familysearch.org/catalog/search.

The page defaults to a place/location search. Enter the country, state, and county where your ancestor lived or resided at the time of their enlistment or the place they resided at the end of the war. Here are a few examples:

United States, Michigan, Hillsdale
United States, Georgia, Habersham
United States, Iowa, Clayton

Examining the topics listed for each search result, you may or may not find World War I records listed initially on the page. Record information is sometimes buried under a broader topic. So lets take a look at the results for each of our examples:

United States, Michigan, Hillsdale - Military Records - World War, 1914-1918
Record of Hillsdale County Soldiers and Sailors in Service During the World War
Author: Daughters of the American Revolution. Ann Gridley Chapter (Michigan)

United States, Georgia, Habersham - Military Records - World War, 1914-1918
Discharge Records, 1913-1964
Author: Georgia. Superior Court (Habersham County)

United States, Iowa, Clayton - Military Records
Soldier's Discharge Records, 1865-1948
Author: Clayton County (Iowa). County Recorder

Clicking on each title will reveal more information on each item, as well as its availability to conduct further research online or to place it on a watch list for future research. Where some items may be digitized, they may only be available to view at a FamilySearch Center or a FamilySearch Affiliated site such as a library or archive in the area.

Taking a look at the records from Hillsdale County, the beginning half of the collection (A-O) are limited to microfilm, while the last half (P-Z) are available to view and download from the comfort of your own home.

Meanwhile, the Habersham Georgia are tantalizingly complete but are still waiting to be digitized. It would be worthwhile to see if a FamilySearch Center in that county would be interested in doing a lookup and sending the items you need directly by e-mail. Its also important to note that if you have ancestors from this county who may have served in World War II or Korea to add this to a future research checklist.

The records for Clayton County Iowa encompass both World War I and World War II, with a handy index to help narrow your search to a specific volume and page number. Given the lock and key symbols associated on each record set, these file are locked down to the immediate public. While these records are not available at home, they can be accessed online by making a visit to a local FamilySearch Center or FamilySearch Affiliate location.

Taking a look at an example found in the intriguing set of Hillsdale County, Michigan records entitled *Soldiers and Sailors in Service During the World War*.

Examine Records and add this information to your checklist:
- Birth Date and Place of Birth
- Name of Parents and Place of Residence
- Occupation before Service
- Name and Place of Military Training Camp
- Rank, Company, and Regiment Information
- Transfers and Promotions
- Service Details Battles/Offensives Fought
- Special Skills or Commendations
- Name of Wife/Wives and Children

Add to Checklist or Double Check:
- Name
- Date and Place of Birth

- Enlistment and Discharge Date
- Inconsistencies or Differences in Service Details

In this one record, a researcher would have not only have a reasonably concise account of family details (birth, marriage, occupation, names of parents), it also provides a condensed version of information provided in a full military service record. Access to record is free and available online, and can be downloaded, printed, and integrated into your research project with a minimum of fuss. This one non-federal record punches straight through the perceived brick wall of World War I research, and all that was required was a little digging, a little browsing, and access to the full FamilySearch site.

Fold3

There are a number of genealogists who are ambivalent to using the resources on Fold3. To some folks, the site seems like a cash grab on behalf of the sites owner Ancestry.com. Why choose to place military records on the Fold3 site when Ancestry.com already has a perfectly great user portal. Other researchers don't particularly care for the user interface, finding the search features too difficult or confusing to operate.

One of the best strategies for using Fold3 is to stay away from the main search box at the top of the page. Click on the browse tab at the top of the website header. This will take you to a full category listing of the site, which is broken down by war/conflict by date followed by a listing for non-military records. The Fold3 site unfolds like an accordion, and by selecting World War I, the site will expand to a publication list of sixty-six titles. Notice that when you click on a publication title, the grey search box above the accordion area changes. Each time you click on a specific category, publication, etc, the grey search box refines the search parameters to match your current browsing area. By using this combination of browsing and smart searching, you will become more familiar with the records on the site and narrow your search in each publication title significantly.

As there are ton of different Great War resources from all over the world available on this list, here are most of the record sets available for you to use for US research:

- *Army Registers, 1798-1969*
- *Connecticut WWI Service Rosters*
- *Foreign Burial of American War Dead*
- *Gorrell's History - AEF Air Service*
- *Naturalization Index - WWI Soldiers*
- *Navy and Marine Corps Officer Registers*
- *Navy Casualty Reports, 1776-1941*
- *Navy Cruise Books, 1918-2009*
- *New York 74th Regiment Service Cards*
- *New York State Adjutant General Reports, 1846-1995*
- *New York State Military Museum Photos (Civil War - Vietnam War)*
- *Ohio, Soldiers Grave Registration Cards, 1804-1958*
- *Rendezvous Reports Index - WWI Armed Guard Personnel*
- *US Army WWI Transport Service, Passenger Lists*
- *US Expeditionary Force, North Russia*
- *US Veterans Administration Pension Payment Cards*
- *Veterans Affairs BIRLS Death File*
- *WWI - State Dept Records*
- *WWI Draft Registration Cards*
- *WWI Military Cablegrams - AEF and War Dept*
- *WWI New York Army Cards*
- *WWI Officer Experience Reports - AEF*
- *WWI Panoramic Unit Photos*

The following items on this site to be exceptionally helpful in acquiring information on individual men and women serving in the Great War.

Army Registers, 1798-1969

Army registers are a great tool for tracing enlisted personnel in the US Army in three key years. Although not every single person serving in the US Army in 1916, 1918, and 1920 is listed, this record collection probably one of the biggest compilations of military service available online and in a readily accessible format. The registers generally contain information relating to the enlistment and termination of service of enlisted personnel.

This register includes quite a bit of in-depth information for each enlisted person including
- Name
- Rank
- Date of Rank
- Highest Brevet Rank
- Previous Service Information & Dates of Promotion and Advancement
- Birth Date and Place of Birth

Connecticut WWI Service Rosters

These service rosters are another collateral source which provides a huge amount of information in a compact fashion. Similar to the examples found in Hillsdale, Michigan earlier in the chapter, this resource stretches out to encompass the entirety of the state, and gives researchers a snapshot of Connecticut servicemen during the great wary. Arranged alphabetically by city, veterans are listed A-Z for each location.

This roster includes quite a bit of in-depth information for each enlisted person including
- Name
- Serial Number
- Address
- Enlistment Place and Date
- Rank
- Company, Regiment, Unit Information
- Training Camp Location and Dates
- Dates of Military Service abroad
- Discharge Date
- Notable Citations

WWI New York Army Cards

New York has the reputation among genealogists for being one of the worst states to request records or conduct genealogy research. Part of this reputation stems from the lackluster availability of even the most basic vital records coupled with the states continuous actions to block access to public records. So it was exceptionally surprising to discover the depth and extensive information is available online for individual Great War soldiers. Fold3 is an essential site to anyone researching World War I ancestors due to its almost instantaneous availability of essential information.

Taking a look at the *WWI New York Army Cards* on Fold3, the title is more than a little misleading. This isnt just a collection of US Army information, this title also contains well organized card collections for Army Nurses, Marines, Navy personnel, and officers. This is the first place to go for New York WWI research, and it is truly exceptional. The cards corresponding to Army nurses are especially important, as they provide a stunning amount of information on personnel who served not only abroad but of those nurses who served in hospitals and facilities on the home front.

These cards include quite a bit of in-depth information for each individual which includes:
- Name
- Serial number
- Race
- Address
- Birthplace and date of birth
- Induction or enlistment place and date
- Name of Training Camp
- Organizations and staff assignments
- Military engagements
- Wounds received in action
- Dates served overseas
- Discharge Date
- Citizenship status
- Remarks

It is important to note that the two additional New York collections in the World War I category, *New York State Adjutant General Reports, 1846-1995* and *New York State Military Museum Photos (Civil War - Vietnam War)* should not be overlooked in your search. Search each collection carefully and you may find additional information or photographs of your ancestor. These items will not appear in a typical online search. Also, make a note to revisit these two other collections later in your research should you need additional information or resources.

WWI Panoramic Unit Photos

In your search for dates and facts pertaining to your Great War ancestor, you may overlook one of the best and often overlooked features of the Fold3 site the free World War I collection of panoramic photographs. Again, the title is deceiving, as the name implies a collection of wide angle photographs of landscapes and battlefields. This simply isnt the case. Yes, there are amazing images of the training camps, warships, and far off places. The site also includes a vast assessment of regimental and corps photographs online. The best part all these photos are free to view and download without a Fold3 subscription. The names of the regiments can be very vague, and there are a number of unknown photographs as well which are worth checking out. As you collect company and unit information, youll want to browse through the Fold3 collection of Great War photographs to see if your ancestor is featured in some of the amazing unit photos. Youll be amazed at what youll find!

A few gems from this collection:

3rd Infantry, Company B (Missouri)
The photograph of this Missouri unit not only has a date (August 10, 1917), each man is numbered and their initials and/or surname are featured on the back of the item. This is a fantastic bonus and gives an identity to everyone posing in the image. BONUS: Use Missouri photographs in conjunction with the Missouri Over There website - http://missourioverthere.org/.

35th Division, Kansas National Guard, Field Hospital Number 2
In a photograph taken in Parsons, Kansas on September 7, 1917, this determined group of men is pictured with their canine mascot sleeping in the front row

89th Division, 353rd Infantry, Company B
This image adds additional details of service for the men serving in this company. The bottom of the photo states 'Sailed for Foreign Service June

4th 1918 Arrived in US May 22 1919'. You can add this information or double check this fact with your research checklist.

Internet Archive

Internet Archive contains an immense and growing collection of digitized genealogy resources located in libraries and archives from around the world. Resources can be read online, or downloaded to a variety of e-readers and tablets. This site is a great example of using library sources for your World War I research, and there are quite a few local, state, and national resources available.

Here are a few examples:
Soldiers of the Great War by Frank G. Howe and Alfred C. Doyle
- Volume 1 https://archive.org/details/SoldiersOfTheGreatWarV1
- Volume 2 https://archive.org/details/SoldiersOfTheGreatWarV2
- Volume 3 https://archive.org/details/SoldiersOfTheGreatWarV3

While the Great War was winding down, Frank G. Howe and Alfred C. Doyle coordinated an effort to collect all the names and photograph of the US military veterans who had died during service. The effort took into account military death bulletins, and a herculean effort to provide photographs of each of the deceased. Photographs were collected by the author from family, friends, educational facilities, and members of the American Red Cross. As space allowed, they included veterans who were wounded in action, but survived the war. Information and photographs of enlisted nurses are also included in these books, which made these publications progressive and comprehensive at the time of their release.

Their efforts produced three books which are essential browsing for WWI researchers. In each volume, the official list of war dead for each county has been listed in some type of alphabetical format of each person by state, rank, and manner of death. The only other information provided is each solider or nurses city or area of residence.

The photographs did not follow this strict pattern. They are separated by state, but are not listed in any particular order. It will be necessary to browse the photographs for each state to find a photo of a veteran.

Each photo includes an abbreviation for type of death or alive with injury:
- K.A. Killed in Action
- D.D. Died of Disease
- D.W. Died of Wounds
- D.A. Died of Accident
- W.A. Wounded in Action

Here a quote from the introduction regarding the availability of photographs in the publication:

"We soon learned that it would be impossible to obtain the photographs of all the soldiers who died in the Great War. Many left no photographs, the relatives of many others were reluctant to part with the picture they had, and in some cases conditions were met most unfavorable to the enterprise, but with an abiding faith in the value of this record to the relatives and friends of the departed soldiers, and to the public as historical record, the association continued its labors with an increasing success. The collection of materials continued for a period of over one year, during which time they were made ready for publication."

It is important to note, that while every effort was made to for accuracy, some men and women who died during the Spanish Flu epidemic whilst in military service in 1919 are not listed in this publication. I've also seen a few misspelled names as well. If you cannot find a deceased or wounded veteran by state, look under the appendix section in the third volume of the series.

Honor Roll Books

Some of the new and exciting items being added to the Internet Archive collection are a series of Great War honor roll publications printed in the 1920s. In the years following the war, Leader Publishing Company in Pipestone, Minnesota offered communities a way to commemorate veterans of the Great War (both living and dead) in a printed book format. The company designed a book which communities could submit veteran service details and their photographs by mail and receive an excellent and detailed publication in return. These books are formulaic by design, however, they contain details and photographs for nearly every veteran in each county. Here are a few examples of some of the titles available on Internet Archive:

- *An Honor Roll Containing a Pictorial Record of the Gallant and Courageous Men from Pipestone County, Minn., U.S.A., Who Served in the Great War, 1917-1918-1919* https://goo.gl/MY6hV8
- *An Honor Roll Containing a Pictorial Record of the Gallant and Courageous Men from Ontonagon County, Mich., U.S.A., Who Served in the Great War. 1917--1918-1919* https://goo.gl/6kogGV
- *An Honor Roll Containing a Pictorial Record of the Gallant and Courageous Men from Montgomery County, Illinois, U.S.A., Who Served in the Great War, 1917-1918-1919* https://goo.gl/wi2qde
- *An Honor Roll Containing a Pictorial Record of the Gallant and Courageous Men from Nobles County, Minn., U. S. A., Who Served in the Great War, 1917-1918-1919* https://goo.gl/9tg8Ef
- *An Honor Roll Containing a Pictorial Record of the Gallant and Courageous Men from Rock County, Minn., U. S. A., Who Served in the Great War, 1917-1918-1919* https://goo.gl/5yKKss
- An Honor Roll Containing a Pictorial Record of the Gallant and Courageous Men from Whitman County, Washington, U. S. A., Who Served in the Great War, 1917-1918-1919 https://goo.gl/2Yo4Gp

There are additional county honor roll books by this publisher available on Internet Archive, however, they do not match the above titles exactly.

- *The Honor Roll, Gibson County, Tennessee, U. S. A., 1917-1918-1919* https://goo.gl/551EGF
- *The Honor Roll 1917--1918--1919 Bureau County, Illinois* https://goo.gl/qnaW9A
- *An Honor Roll : Containing a Pictorial Record of the War Service of the Men and Women of Kalamazoo County, 1917-1918-1919* https://goo.gl/AdZR55
- *Honor Roll, 1917-1918-1919, Jasper County, Iowa in the World*

War : a History of One County's Loyalty in the Struggle for World Democracy https://goo.gl/TquK1P
- *In the World War : Fillmore County, Minnesota* https://goo.gl/g2SDFp

The honored dead from each county are placed in the first pages of the book, followed by photographs and service information for living veterans. Each man and woman are in alphabetical order by military branch and include Army, Navy, National Guard, and military corps nurses.

These books also contain collections of informal photographs taken at home and abroad. Nearly all these photographs contain names of people and their designated placement in each image.

Most importantly, these county honor roll books contain additional images and information for non-combatants such as Red Cross Volunteers, Liberty Loan Committee Members, Home Guard Volunteers, Community Band members, American Legion commanders, and much more. FamilySearch offers a small collection of these books both online and in a physical format as well. You can find their listings here: https://goo.gl/ZrrYjz. As this publisher generated book orders from all over the United States, the county you need for your research may not be online. If you cannot find a county honor roll book listing on http://www.worldcat.org, visit your local library, archive, historical society, museum, or genealogical society for assistance.

Here some examples of additional World War titles which contain genealogical information for researchers:

- *Honor Roll and Complete War History of Genesee County, Michigan, in the Great World War 1914 to 1918*
- *Tippecanoe County Honor Roll: Containing Photographs and Biographical Notes of the Men and Women from Tippecanoe County, Both in the Army, Navy and Marines, Together with their Achievements and Gallant Deeds in the Great World Conflict*
- *World War Roll of Honor, 1917-1920, Marion County, Kansas*
- *The Roll of Honor for Otsego County, New York*

- *Gold Star Honor Roll. A Record of Indiana Men and Women who Died in the Service of the United States and the Allied Nations in the World War. 1914-1918*
- *Yonkers in the World War, Including the Honor Roll of the Citizens of Yonkers who served in the Military Forces of the United States During the World War. With a Record of Overseas and Home Activities During the War Period, of the City of Yonkers as a Community*
- *Madison County's (NY) Welcome Home for her Sons and Daughters who Served in the World War from 1917 to 1919: With a Complete Roster, a List of Golden Stars, and Special Articles*
- *Menard County Honor Book: an Honorary Roll of those Who Took Part in the World War in behalf of the Citizens of Menard County. Petersburg, Athens, Greenview, Tallula, Cantrall, Oakford, Atterbury, Fancy Prairie, Tice, Sweetwater in Illinois*

Additional Books and Resources Online

When piecing together your ancestors journey, it is important to collect not only the individual details of their service, but to branch out and collect location and experience information as well. For many of the young men and women serving in the armed forced, the Great War was an experience unlike few others in their lives. They may have left home or the family farm for the first time, or they may have traveled extensively to receive specialized training. The communal shared experience inherent in the military at the time placed people from different socioeconomic, cultural, and geographic backgrounds together on a grand scale. Experiences during youth shape our world view, and in the rush to find military service details you may overlook aspects of your ancestors overall journey.

Hathi Trust

Hathi Trust brings together a multimillion digital book collection online using resources from Google Books, Internet Archive, and other participating institutions. While there are some shortcomings with this site regarding availability of accessing all items listed, it is a great place to search for titles and resources which span both genealogical and historical records.

Here are a few examples of what you can find on the site:
- *"Dear Folks at Home -" The Glorious Story of the United States Marines in France as told by their Letters from the Battlefield*
- *War Diary of 354th Infantry; Missouri, Kansas, Nebraska, Colorado, Wisconsin, Illinois*
- *The World War Honor Roll of Those South Carolinians, Who Entering the Services from their State, Died While Serving in the Armed Forces of the United States*
- *From Harlem to the Rhine; the Story of New York's Colored Volunteers*
- *The World War and Historic Deeds of Valor from Official Records and Illustrations of the United States and Allied Governments; History of Wars in Which the United States has Participated Volume 6*

The National World War I Museum and Memorial Online

Museums are one of the underutilized sources for genealogical research. When the Liberty Memorial Museum was opened its doors to the public in 1926, its sheer existence was made possible by a flood of public donations and support to keep the memory of Great War veterans relevant and vibrant for the generations to come. The museum collected a prodigious amount of items, books, artifacts, newspapers, private papers, and photographs during its lifetime. Designated as America's official World War I museum in 2004, the site was renamed the National World War I Museum and Memorial. In addition to an expansive remodeling, a huge effort was made to make private diaries, correspondence, photographs, and other collections available online and searchable. It is important to note, that while there is an extensive online collection, it is still only a fraction of what is available in physical format.

You can begin a search of the collection by visiting https://www.theworldwar.org/explore/online-collections-database. One of the best aspects of using the site is using the search by term feature of the catalog search. The search by term page provides a compiled people list by surname, which allows for quick and easy browsing. Couple this feature with the search terms and subjects, and you have a great way to find information without having to resort to endless search browsing. During your search of the online catalog, keep your terms very simple!

Here are a few items available online:

- Final unit rosters listing names and addresses of individual soldiers
- Rare and unique photographs of men and women on the front lines, in recreation camps, and on leave in Europe
- Published unit histories including photographs and personal information of soldiers
- Personal correspondence, letters, and official government memos
- Unit or regimental reunion photographs taken after the Great War

As items were donated to the museum by individuals or families, this provides a great opportunity to explore the collection from a specific regiment or unit. Take this example items donated by Sergeant (Wilhelm) August Heineman, who served with Section 3 Group "A" of the 328th Motor Transport Corps contains photographs of individuals from his unit, views from the battlefield, scenes from the motor repair parks, and dog mascots, as well as souvenir tourist maps of Paris, prayer books, and camp newspapers.

Remember, people do not live their lives in a solitary bubble. They have friends, family, acquaintances, co-workers, and fellow men-at-arms around them during their lifetime. A genealogist looking for information and photographs for an ancestor serving in the 328th Motor Transport Corps could browse the photographs looking for their ancestor, utilize the information found in the camp newspaper, and incorporate the scenes from the repair parks and camp areas into their research.

If you cant find items online, send the archive and museum staff a reference request for the unit/regiment/corps you need. Visit https://www.theworldwar.org/explore/edward-jones-research-center for more information.

Newspapers

Newspapers can fill an enormous gap in tracing your Great War ancestors. From small communities to large cities, the local paper printed pictures and details of an individuals military service. Parents and siblings sent information on their doughboy to newsrooms across the country, and everything from personal letters to casualty lists were printed every day during the war period. If you had more than one ancestor, lets say your grandfather and his three brothers, who enlisted or were drafted into service, a local reporter would more than likely take the time to highlight each man and their commitment to the country.

Newspaper access is spread between digital, physical, and microfilm formats. While there is not a one stop location to begin your newspaper research, there are several online sites, both free and available through subscription, which can be accessed from the comfort of your home. Take a moment to search for a state or university sponsored newspaper collection online, as these sites can be overlooked in the rush to subscribe to a paid subscription service.

Free Newspaper Sites
- Chronicling America - https://chroniclingamerica.loc.gov/
- Old Fulton Postcards - http://fultonhistory.com/Fulton.html
- Google News Archive - https://news.google.com/newspapers
- Elephind - https://elephind.com/
- Bowling Green State University - http://libguides.bgsu.edu/USNewspapersInternet

Great Sites with Links to Free and Paid Publications
- ICON Newspaper Digitization Projects - http://icon.crl.edu/digitization.php
- Ancestor Hunt Newspaper Research Links - http://www.theancestorhunt.com/newspaper-research-links.html#.Wr0ihi7waUk

Things to look for during newspaper research:
- Draft lists
- Enlistments
- Troop Movements
- Furloughs
- Casualty Lists (Both Dead and Wounded)
- Private Letters from Servicemen and Women to their Families
- Social News (Births, Marriages, Deaths)

- Articles Highlighting Military Service of Siblings Serving Abroad
- Send Off and Welcome Home Parades/Ceremonies
- Articles Mentioning Specific People and Units after Military Service

American Legion Magazine Archive
https://archive.legion.org/handle/20.500.12203/4695

The American Legion was founded at the end of World War I. As veterans settled into life back in the states, the legion magazine provides articles on veterans topics, as well as details on life events from their subscribers. One of the best sections for genealogists is called *Buddies in Distress*, where groups or individuals place printed requests for information on specific people. One example of a *Buddies in Distress* listing is the following: "Fletcher, George Rowe. Corp., 333d Motor Truck Co., discharged April, 1919. from Camp McClellan, Ala. Anyone knowing this man's present location please advise."

The online archive is organized by decade for easy browsing, and each individual issue offers a list of articles on an information page, as well as a link to the downloadable PDF copy of each magazine. This is a full and complete collection, with every magazine printed available for free to download and use for your research.

Trench Journals and Unit Magazines of the First World War
http://microsite.proquest.com/page/trench

Just as traditional newspapers provide details on service men and women on the home front, there were a bevy of publications created by units, troops, corps, hospitals, civilian service organizations, and prisoners of war. In addition to articles, publications may include soldier biographies, staff highlights, unit jokes, charitable efforts, and news from home. Trench Journals and Unit Magazines of the First World War is a subscription-based site which can be accessed from a large college or university, as well as specialized archives and libraries. All the publications on the site are downloadable and provide source citations for your research. A few of the publications on this site include *The Dead Horse Corner Gazette*, *The Iodine Chronicle*, *Steering Wheel*, *Church Army*, and *Soldiers Wives and Mothers' League*. Do not overlook this site as a resource! Contact your nearest university library and inquire as to the availability of this database.

Camp Books

Training camps provided the first exposure to military service, and they were ranged from established bases to hastily created spaces dotted with wood structures and a sea of tents. There are several sources you can use to discover the location and dates of your ancestors training camp experience.
- Federal Military Service Record
- State Military Service Card
- Veterans Bonus Claim Records
- Federal Muster Roll
- County Honor Rolls
- Private Correspondence

When you have the name and location of the camp, you can begin browsing and search for details on training camp experiences. Many camps books were published both officially and unofficially in the years following the war. These books contain quite a bit of information on the daily activities, special events, housing conditions, company/regiment/unit information, maps, and a wide variety of photographs. You can find information on camps which do not currently have a published book by conducting research at state and local archives where the camp was located.

Here are a few examples of training camp books available online:
- *Camp Dix* https://goo.gl/Vc4eVS
- *The Birth of Camp Jackson* https://goo.gl/zqZGsi
- *Camp Upton* https://goo.gl/QDaCAx
- *Camp Travis and it's Part in the World War* https://goo.gl/KuXL2H
- *The Ninety-First, the First at Camp Lewis* https://goo.gl/ciyY5e

The World War I Centennial Commission

Part of the mission of the World War I Centennial Commission is to provide a space for each state to highlight links and resources pertaining to their own personal records and history of the Great War. Each state committee has used their own website space to create a landing page which is unique and reflective of their location. These sites can range from a collection of regularly updated blog posts highlighting new exhibits and archival material or serve as an educational resource site complete with a list of recommended speakers, topics, and downloadable items.

You can browse through the map of the project at http://www.worldwar1centennial.org/index.php/participate/state-organizations/state-websites/others-pending.html

The main commission website is updated regularly and includes a sign up page for weekly dispatches, a podcast series, press releases, and updates on the new national World War I monument in Washington D.C.

Chapter 3 - State Specific Collections and Resources

To help connect researchers to the wealth of information available on a localized level, several state-wide projects have been developed their own Great War genealogy and history websites and made access to records readily available to the public. Not all the records you need for your research are available online, so you do not want to skip over traditional brick and mortar resources available by mail from state archives or other depositories. Depending on your veteran's state of residence, these non-digital resources are absolutely essential.

It is also important to note that while this chapter may seem extensive, it does not account for every resource available for every state. The links and information provided will give you a starting point for your research, and whenever possible, information on essential records such as service cards, discharges, and honor rolls have been included. County honor roll books, war histories by county, and other book-based items may or may not be included in this collection, so check for local resources whenever possible.

Alabama
Alabama Department of Archives and History
- *World War I Service Cards, Gold Star Database, War Deaths, and Administrative Files* http://www.archives.alabama.gov/referenc/military.html#World%20War%20I

Ancestry.com
- Alabama, WWI Gold Star Index, 1917-1918

***

Alaska
Alaska State Archives
- *Service Personnel Information*
- *Number of Service Members by Community*
- *Death Statistics*

http://archives.alaska.gov/for_researchers/coll_guides.html

Arizona
FamilySearch.org
- Military Discharges & Enrollment Records (Various by County) https://goo.gl/WdAHC3

Arkansas
Arkansas and the Great War Digital Collections
https://www.butlercenter.org/arkansas-and-the-great-war

Arkansas State Archives (off line collections)
- Arkansas Veterans of World War I papers, World War I collection, and World War I Discharge Records https://goo.gl/mDVU9g

California
California Goes to War
https://goo.gl/2qE5w7

Ancestry.com
- *California, WWI Soldier Service Cards, 1917-1918*
- *California, World War I Death Announcements, 1918-1921*
- *California, World War I Soldier Citations, 1918-1921*
- *California, WWI Soldier Photographs, 1917-1918*

Colorado
FamilySearch.org
- Military Discharges, Discharge Certificates & Birth Information (Various by County) https://goo.gl/x4JH1N

Connecticut
Connecticut in World War I
http://ctinworldwar1.org/

Connecticut Digital Archive
http://collections.ctdigitalarchive.org

FamilySearch.org
- *Service records : Connecticut Men and Women in the Armed forces of the United States During World War, 1917-1920* https://www.familysearch.org/search/catalog/2840512

Delaware
Delaware's Role in World War I
https://history.delaware.gov/exhibits/online/WWI/Delaware-role-ww1.shtml

The Delaware Public Archives (offline collections)
https://archives.delaware.gov/
- World War I Servicemen Records
- World War I Army Service Record Cards

Florida
Florida in World War I
https://www.floridamemory.com/exhibits/wwi

FamilySearch.org
- Military Discharges (Various by County) https://goo.gl/cE6Lux

Georgia
FamilySearch.org
- Army and Navy Discharge Records, World War I Military Service Files (Various by County) https://goo.gl/otBzM4

Hawaii

Internet Archive
- Hawaii in the World War https://archive.org/details/ahb2432.0001.001.umich.edu

Idaho
FamilySearch.org
- Military Discharges, Discharge Certificates & Birth Information (Various by County) https://goo.gl/NPp4Vg

Illinois
Illinois Digital Archives
http://www.idaillinois.org/cdm/landingpage/collection/isl8

FamilySearch.org
- Honor Rolls, Service Cards, Discharge Records, and Veteran Burials (Various by County) https://goo.gl/9PFB8b

Illinois State Archives (offline collections)
- *Service Recognition Board: World War I Bonus Applications from Veteran's and Beneficiaries, 1923-1927*
- *Military and Naval Department: World War I Bonus Correspondence, 1932-1955*

Indiana
Indiana Digital Archives
- Indiana The Gold Star Honor Roll and the Book of Merit Databases https://secure.in.gov/apps/iara/search/Home/Search?RecordSeriesId=3

Indiana Archives and Records Administration (off line collections)
https://www.in.gov/iara/3201.htm
- World War I Service Cards

Iowa
Iowa in the Great War
http://iagenweb.org/greatwar/

FamilySearch.org

- Military Discharges, Honor Rolls, and Gold Star Records (Various by County) https://goo.gl/9PFB8b

Kansas
Kansas WWI
https://www.kansasww1.org

Kansas State Historical Society
- Kansas WWI Military Records - https://www.kshs.org/p/military-records-world-war-i/11201

Ancestry.com
- *Kansas, Camp Funston Military Records, 1914-1919*
- *Kansas, World War I Veteran Collection, 1917-1919*

FamilySearch.org
- Discharge Records, and Veteran Burials (Various by County) https://goo.gl/3QXcVQ

Kentucky
Kentucky Department for Libraries and Archives
- WWI Military Service Cards and Veterans Bonus Claim Records (offline collections) http://www.orderfirstworldwar.com/kentucky-service-cards.htm WWI Service Cards and Veteran's Bonus applications are available by request in person or by mail at the Kentucky Department for Libraries and Archives in Frankfort. To save time, request the service card and the veteran's bonus application records on separate pages. As an important note, the Veteran's Bonus Claim records are not listed in the form's drop down menu, so write in 'WWI Veteran's Bonus Claim' in the box. The fee for each record is $10 for state residents, $15 for non-KY residents, and can be requested by mail using a handy downloadable form. The library and archives service staff are very friendly and helpful by phone if you have any questions or need help filling out your request form - https://kdla.ky.gov/researchers/Documents/military.pdf

Louisiana
FamilySearch.org
- State World War I Military Service Cards https://goo.gl/rdfZRn
- Veterans Lists, Casualty Lists, Discharges, and Veteran Obituaries by Parish https://goo.gl/7Cm4BC

Maine
FamilySearch.org
- *WWI Soldiers Index by Town*   https://goo.gl/MnsEk8
- WWI Grave Cards, WWI Draft Registration Index, National Guard Service Cards and more   https://goo.gl/tBggDn

Maryland
FamilySearch.org
- Maryland in the World War, 1917-1919 : Military and Naval Service Records https://goo.gl/Bd8r3D

Massachusetts
FamilySearch.org
- Limited service files and service cards (Various by County) https://goo.gl/8396oR

Michigan
FamilySearch.org
- Honor Rolls and Compiled Service Cards (Various by County) https://goo.gl/fJhAX9
- Michigan County War Records, 1917-1919 : Census of Men Serving in U.S. Forces   https://goo.gl/WHj6Yo

Archives of Michigan (offline records)
- *Veterans' Bonus Files, 1921-1953*
- *Census of World War I Veterans, 1917-1919*
- *WWI Research Guide* http://seekingmichigan.org/wp-content/uploads/2017/01/4d-WorldWarI.pdf

Minnesota
FamilySearch.org

- *Minnesota, Military Records : World War I Bonus Files and Service Records, 1918-1943* https://goo.gl/954AeP
- Gold Star Rolls, Service Records by Surname, Veteran's Bonus Files https://goo.gl/yVuWUB

Mississippi
FamilySearch.org
- Service Files and Service Cards (Various by County) https://goo.gl/jZvzkG
- Master Alphabetical Index, World War Veterans, Army, 1917-1918 https://goo.gl/rmkAdC

Missouri
Missouri 'Over There'
http://missourioverthere.org/service-database/

FamilySearch.org
- Service Files and Service Cards (Various by County) https://goo.gl/BC8SWg

Montana
Montana Memory Project
- WWI Military and Nurses Service Enlistment Cards https://goo.gl/DDJhUx

FamilySearch.org
- Military Rolls, Honor Rolls, and Service Record Books (Various by County) https://goo.gl/wuBHfj

Nebraska
Nebraska State Historical Society
- Nebraska World War I Commemoration https://veterans.nebraska.gov/WWI

FamilySearch.org
- Rosters of WWI Service (Various by County) https://goo.gl/3V7k4J

Nevada
FamilySearch.org
- Gold star rolls, and Veteran Birth Year Information (Various by County) https://goo.gl/QFUjp7

New Hampshire
FamilySearch.org
- *New Hampshire, World War I Certificates of Service* https://goo.gl/4JEvT2
- *Master Alphabetical Index, World War Veterans, Army, 1917-1918* https://goo.gl/tHTTYf

New Jersey
New Jersey Department of State
- World War I Deaths https://goo.gl/Bg9WxK

New Mexico
Ancestry.com
- *New Mexico, World War I Records, 1917-1919*

New York
New York State Military Museum
- New York World War I Units https://dmna.ny.gov/historic/reghist/wwi/

Ancestry.com
- *New York 74th Regiment Service Cards*
- *New York State Adjutant General Reports, 1846-1995*
- *New York State Military Museum Photos (Civil War - Vietnam War)*
- *WWI New York Army Cards*

North Carolina
FamilySearch.org
- *North Carolina, World War I Service Cards, 1917-1919* https://www.familysearch.org/search/collection/2568864
- Military Discharge Records (Various by County) https://goo.gl/

UEJjkY

North Dakota
State Historical Society of North Dakota
- North Dakota and the Great War http://history.nd.gov/wwi/

Ohio
Ancestry.com
- *Ohio Soldiers in WWI, 1917-1918*

FamilySearch.org
- Military Discharge Records (Various by County) https://goo.gl/3Wns3S

Oklahoma
FamilySearch.org
- Military Discharge Records (Various by County) https://goo.gl/w8B66N

Oregon
Oregon Secretary of State
- Oregon at War http://sos.oregon.gov/archives/exhibits/ww1/Pages/default.aspx

FamilySearch.org
- Soldiers Registers and Military Discharge Records (Various by County) https://goo.gl/2SdCfT

Oregon Secretary of State (offline collections)
- World War I Personal Service History Records http://sos.oregon.gov/archives/Pages/records/genealogy/record-types.aspx

Pennsylvania
FamilySearch.org
Military Discharge Records (Various by County) https://goo.gl/ir6mP4

* * *

Rhode Island
Rhode Island Department of State
- RI National Guard Pay Rolls http://sos.ri.gov/archon/?p=digitallibrary/digitalcontent&id=416

FamilySearch.org
- Honor Rolls and State Militia Lists (Various by County) https://goo.gl/zCX4UN

South Carolina
South Carolina State Library Digital Collections
- *The Official Roster of South Carolina Soldiers, Sailors and Marines in the World War, 1917-18* https://dc.statelibrary.sc.gov/handle/10827/9425

South Dakota
Ancestry.com
- *North Dakota Military Men*

FamilySearch.org
- Honor Rolls, Casualty Lists, and Military Deaths Abroad https://goo.gl/ERZZkd

North Dakota State Archives (off line collections)
- Division Pamphlets, American Legion Biographic Sketches, Photographs, Private Diaries and much more https://history.sd.gov/archives/military.aspx

Tennessee
FamilySearch.org
- Honor Rolls and Military Discharges (Various by County) https://goo.gl/vEixAz

Tennessee State Archives (offline collections)
- Service Cards, Veteran Questionnaires, Gold Star Mothers and Widows Questionnaires, Private Correspondence, Division Scrapbooks and much more https://goo.gl/ywJHAq

***

Texas
FamilySearch.org
- *Texas, World War I records, 1917-1920* https://goo.gl/vJPZyn

Utah
Ancestry.com
- *Utah, Military Records, 1861-1970*
- *Utah, Veterans with Federal Service Buried in Utah, 1847-1966*

Vermont
Internet Archive
- *Roster of Vermont Men and Women in the Military and Naval Service of the United States and Allies in the World War, 1917-1919* https://archive.org/details/rosterofvermontm00herb

Vermont State Archives and Records Administration
- World War I Research Guide https://www.sec.state.vt.us/media/828081/vsara-wwi-research-guide.pdf

Virginia
Library of Virginia
- World War I Questionnaires https://goo.gl/kM17dr

FamilySearch.org
- Virginia World War Memorial Records (Various by City and County) https://goo.gl/v2f4qJ

Washington
Washington State Digital Archives
- *World War I Service Statement Cards, 1917-1919* https://www.digitalarchives.wa.gov/Collections/TitleInfo/640

FamilySearch.org
- Honor Rolls and Burial Lists (Various by County) https://goo.gl/gAaCLt
- Katsap and Pierce Counties Citizenship Certificates, Military Enlistments and Discharges https://goo.gl/wKhH84

* * *

West Virginia
West Virginia Division of Culture and History
- West Virginia Veterans Memorial Database http://www.wvculture.org/history/wvmemory/vet.aspx

FamilySearch.org
- West Virginia Military Discharges (Various by County) https://goo.gl/VismzB

Internet Archive
- *West Virginia: Revised List of Deceased Soldiers* https://goo.gl/6yiewz

Wisconsin
University of Wisconsin Madison
- World War I Digital Collection https://uwdc.library.wisc.edu/collections/history/wwicoll

Milwaukee Public Library
- WWI Military Portraits http://content.mpl.org/cdm/landingpage/collection/WWI

FamilySearch.org
- *Registers of Veterans at the National Home for Disabled Volunteer Soldiers, Northwestern Branch in Milwaukee, Wisconsin, 1867-1934* https://goo.gl/EMvz5n
- Honor Rolls, Casualty Rosters, and Gold Star Lists (Various by County) https://goo.gl/v8j9fh

Wisconsin Historical Society (offline collections)
- Wisconsin World War I Service Cards http://www.orderfirstworldwar.com/wisconsin-service-cards.htm

Wyoming
Genealogy Trails
- *Wyoming World War I Casualties from the Soldiers of the Great War* http://genealogytrails.com/wyo/ww1casualties.html

* * *

District of Columbia
Worldcat.org (off line collections)
- *Historical Record and Fiftieth Year Who's Who : District of Columbia Chapter, Military Order of the World Wars : Golden Anniversary Commemoration, 1919-1969* http://www.worldcat.org/title/historical-record-and-fiftieth-year-whos-who-golden-anniversary-commemoration-1919-1969/oclc/117586

Chapter 4 - Examining Essential Records at the National Archives

The National Archives collection of World War I files are spread out over multiple depositories across the country. Here is a short list of some of the records you may wish to use during the course of your research. For a stress-free experience, your goal should be to bring in less than one sheet of paper with you into the research facility as the security protocols are very high. You'll want to rely on a portable battery or charging cord to keep your devices in good working order.

National Archives at St. Louis
The National Personnel Records Center (NPRC)
1 Archives Dr, Saint Louis, MO 63138
Phone: (314) 801-0800
https://www.archives.gov/st-louis

National Archives at St. Louis is also known as the National Personnel Records Center, which is responsible for administering the military service files for individuals who served in 1914 onward. The archives has an extensive microfilm and book collection which is open to researchers without an appointment. If you are requesting original textual records, you will need to schedule an appointment several months in advance and apply for a reader's card. The application process for the reader's card requires a photo ID with proof of address. Set aside about an hour of your time to apply and receive a reader's card.

World War I Records at this depository include:

- **Official Military Personnel Files & Final Payment Voucher Roll (Request form 13173)**
Includes service dates, stations, schooling, transfers, promotions, and decorations.

Use caution when examining information on a final payment voucher. Due to the high number of men being processed out of the service end of the war, your veteran may not have been released in their service unit. Large groups of men comprised of numerous units were processed out in 'discharge detachments', with no mention of their actual service regiment, unit, or corps information. To overcome this stumbling block, refer to other sources such as transportation lists, veteran's bonus claim records, service cards, and county honor roll books to

- **Burial Case Files**
Researching a deceased veteran is sometimes easier than researching someone who survived the war. As individuals died while in service, the military created extensive files regarding each person's initial death and burial. These records do not include information or details of the veteran's death, but they do provide additional information such as dental records, the body's original burial details, and information on how the body was identified. The veteran's next of kin was given the choice to leave the veteran interred in a military cemetery abroad or to transport the body back to the United States for burial. Burial Case Files document initial burials, disinterments, transportation back to the United States, and final burial in a new location. Depending on the individual, a veteran may be buried and transported several times, which perpetuated a fair amount of paperwork.

The US government provided families with the opportunity to visit the burial locations of their loved ones in Europe between 1928 and 1931, which paved the way for the pilgrimages of Gold Star Mothers and Widows from 1930-1933. Burial Case Files include details of these pilgrimages including passport photos and information, health cards, trip itineraries, hotel information, and other the details of the mothers and widows is included. Additional Gold Star Mothers and Widows correspondence and photographs can be found at National Archives II in College Park, Maryland in Record Group (RG) 92 Records of the Office of the Quartermaster General.

- **Court Martial Records**

Accessing court martials is a two-step process. The index to World War I court martials is only available at National Archive II in College Park, Maryland. The physical court martial records are housed at the National Archives in St. Louis. While this confusing, and makes absolutely no sense, it is worth searching the index (or paying/bribing someone to check the index on your behalf), to see if a record for your soldier exists. Court martial records include a detailed list of charges, eye witness testimony and statements from the accused, a copy of general orders/special orders, a charge sheet, a summary of the court record, and a final verdict. Cases can range from going AWOL, drunkenness, robbery, and other smaller charges.

- **Morning reports (available on microfilm)**

These are a great and underutilized set of records. Not only do Morning Reports document a company or unit's physical movements, they also provide remarks on monthly transfers, furloughs, promotions, and hospitalizations. This is an essential tool in plotting your soldier's journey in the US and Europe and can be easily added to mapping software such as Google Maps. These reports may or may not contain individual names, however, it provides a solid account of incidents such as shelling, injuries, and breakouts of disease. These records are free to access on microfilm with no appointment needed.

- **Muster Rolls and Rosters (available on microfilm)**

Muster Rolls and Rosters provide a stunning amount of information on individuals who may not have a surviving Military Personnel Service File. Not only do these files include valuable information such as service numbers, enlistment dates and location, and training camp details, it also documents the names of everyone in each unit from top to bottom. The details in these records vary, but the notes field can include information on hospitalizations, court martials, transfers, and other assignments. It also provides a location and date of where and when the information was documented. Be on the lookout for the final for final muster rolls as there may be additional details which may be of use. Muster Rolls and Rosters are a great tool for contacting and networking with other genealogists who may be able to provide previously unknown photographs and information. These records are free to access on microfilm with no appointment needed.

- **Morning Sick Reports**

These reports contain lists of people hospitalized or quarantined during military service. These are of particular use to anyone who has a family story of an ancestor who died or fell ill during the influenza epidemic of 1918-1920. Lists are arranged by unit and report names of individuals, their disease and condition, and where they are being treated. An appointment with the National Archives is required to view these records.

National Archives at College Park (National Archives II)
8601 Adelphi Road
Phone: 301-837-3510
https://www.archives.gov/dc-metro/college-park/researcher-info.html

Conducting research in person at the National Archives can seem overwhelming, however, by reviewing what type of records are available ahead of time can give you an idea of what you want to browse, and what records look interesting. To save time, search the National Archives Catalog to get an idea of what information is available on a specific unit/regiment/corps and save them to a smart phone or laptop device.

National Archives II offers three four distinct areas of research for genealogists and historians – textual records, photographs, maps, and films. All of which are located in different areas of the archive.

The bulk of World War I records are located in *Record Group 120: Records of the American Expeditionary Forces (World War I), 1848 – 1942*. A full summary of the group is available online at https://www.archives.gov/research/guide-fed-records/groups/120.html. When you arrive at the National Archives, consult with the experts in the research room. They will help you fill out request forms, assist you in searching for records, and make recommendations of items you may not have found in your catalog search. Plan to spend at least two full days of your research trip at the archives learning how to request records and browsing through the in-house archive catalogs.

Historical Reports of Hospitals and Infirmaries, 5/1/1917 - 5/31/1920 consists of inoculation reports, sanitation reports, personnel rosters of doctors and nurses, lists of sick and wounded, and medical statistics relating to U.S. Army hospitals and infirmaries in the United States during World War I.
https://catalog.archives.gov/id/653140

It's important to note that the items in this record group account for less than ten percent of the actual paperwork generated during the war. The National Archives keeps a sampling of information from this time period, so availability of records for your ancestor's unit will vary greatly. A bulk of the records revolve around correspondence, telegrams, cablegrams, reports, and miscellaneous records. While this sounds dry, these records provide a substantial amount of contextual information and insight into what types of duties, warnings, and training your veteran experienced while in service. While these records vary greatly depending on what unit/regiment you're researching, you can expect to find items such as warning memos to staff for driving military vehicles such as cars, trucks, tanks, and motorcycles recklessly while performing service, reminders of proper military protocol, such as saluting officers or wearing uniform clothing correctly, as well as lists of men sent on special missions or service details. Food menus, service park locations, and special training summaries may also be available.

The World War I photograph collection at National Archives II is well worth a visit on its own. Where the textual records require multiple days of orientation and staff assistance, accessing the photograph collection is a straight forward and simple process, using an easy to use finding guide and wonderful staff assistance to request photographs. While some individuals are listed in identified photographs, broaden your search to include as many unit/regiment/corps images as possible, as well as any place name locations you've acquired in the course of your research. Training camps, furlough locations, contests, pageants, and transportation ships also shouldn't be missed.

The map collection at National Archives II offers a wide range of items, and is essential for anyone researching medical units, nursing staff, and logistical service personnel. The map collections range from maps of hospitals, bases, forts, coffee roasters, recreation camps, and transportation routes. Take the time to consult with a member of staff for assistance requesting the collection and set aside about a day browsing items for your research.

During World War I, the U.S. Army Signal Corps documented the activities of American troops at home and abroad. National Archives II is home to a collection of World War I films which are housed on around 990 reels of film. The signal corps captured priceless footage from various battle operations, daily life on the front, tours of facilities, as well as training films. Use the National Archives catalog to view the collection on line. If you wish to view the collection in person, send a list of films you'd like to see by e-mail to archives staff several weeks in advance by e-mailing mopix@nara.gov. Consult with staff regarding the ability to transfer films to DVD. Visit https://www.archives.gov/publications/prologue/2010/summer/frame-film.html for more details.

National Archives and Records Administration (National Archives I)
700 Pennsylvania Avenue, NW
Washington, DC 20408-0001
Phone: (866) 272-6272
https://www.archives.gov/dc-metro/washington

This building is home to American cornerstone documents such as the Declaration of Independence, the Constitution, and the Articles of Confederation. Researchers do not need enter through the tourist entrance at the front of the building, rather, use the researcher entry door at the back of the building facing Pennsylvania Avenue.

Although the bulk of the records in this depository pre-date 1914, there is one important record set researchers will want to use when utilizing this archive. If you are researching ancestors who became American citizen while serving in the war, you may find direct information within *Record Group 393: Records of U.S. Army Continental Commands, 1817 – 1947, Correspondence Relating to Foreign-Born Soldiers,*

7/1918 - 12/1918, otherwise known as "Alien Papers." This record set is separated by training camp, and document names, immigration dates, names prior to naturalization, and other essential information. Depending on whether you ancestor cooperated fully with the naturalization process, they may have been subject to interviews, which may be included in each camp file. An overview of the collection is available online at https://catalog.archives.gov/id/1133918. You can find more information on World War I naturalizations in the next chapter.

Library of Congress
www.loc.gov
The Library of Congress is an overlooked gem for World War I research. Where this depository may not carry the same type of records found at the National Archives, it is well worth the effort to browse through the following resources during your research:
- World War I Photo Collection https://www.loc.gov/photos/?q=World+War+I+Photos
- Camp and Base Newspapers https://www.loc.gov/rr/main/ww1/news-general.html
- Veterans History Project www.loc.gov/vets
- World War I Posters http://www.loc.gov/pictures/collection/wwipos/

When working with the photograph collection on the site, you may run across small thumbnail images on the site which do not offer larger photo files available as a download. Before making a trip to Washington D.C. to retrieve these files, e-mail collection staff for assistance requesting a larger version of the photo you need. Visit http://www.loc.gov/rr/askalib/ask-print.html for more details.

State and Regional Archives
It was the role of each state to administrate and supply capable individuals for military service. Each state's Adjutant General's Office kept copious records on their state units and troops, including National Guard records. This structure gives genealogists and historians another layer of records and information in which to accomplish their research goals. Be aware that while state units and troops which were called up to federal service, they traded their state designation to a US Army

designation. For example, the Illinois 1st Infantry was redesignated the 131st Infantry of the 33rd Division.

While this book cannot account for the whereabouts for each state's adjunct general's office, it is important to note that while states may have published books, archived their World War I files, others may have disposed of records due to space or lost them due a fire or natural disaster.

State Veterans Census and/or State Veterans Bonus Claims

Congress approved the World War Adjusted Compensation Act in May 1924. Each veteran was granted a bonus amount of a dollar for each day of domestic service, up to a maximum of $500, and $1.25 for each day of overseas service, up to a maximum of $625. Amounts of $50 or less were immediately paid. All other amounts were issued as Certificates of Service maturing in 20 years. Record keeping was made at the state level, where the amounts for each veteran was recorded.

As the adjunct general for each state was responsible for organizing military units, supplies, processing discharges, and collecting bonus information for each state, some of these records have survived to the present. These records may be housed directly within state archives or the Adjunct General's office. States which have surviving accounts for Bonus Claims include Kentucky, Michigan, New York, Pennsylvania, and Minnesota. Check with the state where your soldier enlisted or resided to see what bonus claim or veteran's census information is available

Records held at the Adjunct General's office in Illinois suffered heavy damage from a fire, and the burned portions of these records were cut away to form small circles or abstract shapes and refiled.

Regional archives may have collections pertaining to World War I veterans in unlikely places, such as compiled lists of veteran burials, soldier or sailor home records, minutes or items pertaining to American Legion posts, or books and photographs collected before and after the war.

County Courthouses

When veterans returned from military service, they were provided the opportunity to file their military discharge papers safely at the local county courthouse free of charge. This provided a bit of security for the veteran, as it reduced the risk of their paperwork being misplaced, stolen, or lost in natural disaster. County courthouses are by no means immune to acts of God, but instances of courthouse fires had declined when counties began housing records in buildings constructed of brick and stone.

For genealogists, county courthouses may contain World War I records such as:

- Records of enlistments and discharges
- Bonuses paid to soldiers, parents and widows
- Pension records for disabled veterans and widows

Discharge papers are typically filed in the county's grantor indexes, where the paperwork is cited in a volume and page number. The index is a matter of public record, so you should be able to request an index lookup quickly and easily from the office of the county clerk by phone or by e-mail. If your veteran's discharge is available, you can request to see the book directly from the staff either in person or by use of an intermediary.

You will want to pay particular attention to state and county guidelines of who precisely has access to military records on a local level. In the state of Illinois, military discharges records are limited to the veteran who filed them. Parents, spouses, children, grandchildren, and other family members are barred from accessing or requesting them. This is an extreme measure which was meant to protect future military pensions and bonuses of the veteran. However, state and local laws have not been updated, so all military discharges in Illinois, which include all early military discharges from the years before the Civil War and onward are being held hostage from genealogists with no updates to the law in sight.

If you need a discharge from a county with closed access, make a trip to the local Veteran's Administration office for the county in question, and bring your pedigree sheets, proof of kinship, and photo ID with you. The staff at the VA can request the records for you on your behalf with a quick phone call to the office of the county clerk. This is may be a difficult task for a researcher who is residing in another state, however, in this age of e-mail and easy document scanning, contact the local VA office ahead of time by phone and e-mail.

Pritzker Military Museum and Library
104 S. Michigan Ave. 2nd Floor
Chicago, IL 60603
Phone: (312) 374-9333
http://www.pritzkermilitary.org/

In the heart of downtown Chicago, the Pritzker Military Museum and Library is home to a stunning selection of books, photographs, videos, and artifacts documenting the experience of men and women who have served in the armed forces. Their collection consists of over 70,000 items and is a must-visit place for anyone interested in military research. The Pritzker collection is also available through interlibrary loan, so check with your local library to see if they participate in this service. The facility is supported by membership and private donations, with a daily non-member entry fee of $5. The Pritzker staff provide a wide range of knowledge, and the exhibits and lectures hosted at the museum are excellent.

A link to the World War I collection housed at the Pritzker Military Museum and Library can be found online at https://goo.gl/UTtRM4

Cantigny Park First Division Museum and Archives
1S151 Winfield Road
Wheaton, IL 60189
https://www.fdmuseum.org/
P 630.668.5161

The Cantigny Park First Division Museum and Archives is a treat to visit. Not only does the facility offer an outstanding collection of materials and artifacts, the archives staff are proactively working make its expansive array of original materials available in an online digital format. This is a must-visit site for genealogists researching ancestors who served in 'The Fighting First', as well as anyone interested in visiting an outstanding military museum. The main reading room of the archives is available Tuesday through Friday from March to December. Contact the archives staff ahead of your visit whenever possible. If you can't travel to the facility for an in-person visit, the archives portal offers a high caliber of assistance online. Visit https://www.fdmuseum.org/researchers/research-services/ for more information.

List of Additional Research Websites:
US Army Heritage and Education Center - https://ahec.armywarcollege.edu/
Air Force Historical Research Agency - http://www.afhra.af.mil
American Battle Monuments Commission - www.abmc.gov
Europeana - www.europeana.eu
Flanders Field Museum Project - www.inflandersfields.be
Prisoners of the First World War - https://grandeguerre.icrc.org
U.S. National World War I - www.worldwar1centennial.org
Veteran's Oral History Project - www.loc.gov/vets
Library of Congress WWI Collection - www.loc.gov/topics/world-war-i
Brigham Young University World War I Document Archive - http://bit.ly/2wEJ869
Polar Bear Expedition WWI (U.S. Troops in Russia) - http://bit.ly/2wEZQTe
British Library Digital Collections - www.bl.uk/world-war-one

Additional Collections

The Music of the First World War – Illinois Digital Archives
http://idaillinois.org/cdm/search/collection/p16614coll23/page/1
If you're looking for the music soundtrack for the Great War, you'll want to check out the online collection of digitized World War I sheet music and audio uploads available on the Illinois Digital Archive website. This project was funded in part by the Pritzker Military Museum and Library. Andrew Bullen from the Illinois State Library has not only made the digital downloads of over 400 sheet music scores easy and available, he has also created audio files of each piece by using optical music recognition software. Each audio file is programed to emulate the sound of an upright piano found in many middle class homes of the

Great War period. This is a must visit for anyone interested in the popular songs of the First World War.

Online Auction Sites and Vintage Online Retailers
Don't be afraid to look for family items on major sites such as eBay, Etsy, and Cardcow.com. There is an array of World War I items such as identification tags, photographs, albums, uniforms and other materials for sale or by auction. One way to help cut down on the amount of time browsing these sites is to set up a notification system to keep you up to date on what's being added for purchase.

Never Ever Miss Out Again On The Item You Really Want off ebay - https://www.ebay.com/gds/Never-Ever-Miss-Out-Again-On-The-Item-You-Really-Want-/10000000000767264/g.html

5 Ways to Save Time With Etsy's New Listings Manager
https://www.etsy.com/seller-handbook/article/5-ways-to-save-time-with-etsys-new/22851122487

Cardcow.com is a vintage postcard site which offers not only the original post cards for sale, but has high resolution images of each card for purchase as well. While each post card is not searchable by first or last name, cards are searchable by postmark city. Should Cardcow add a first and last name search, as well as an address area to its parameters, it would truly be a much easier site to navigate for genealogists.

Chapter 5 - Naturalization and Enemy Alien Records

There is a unique area research available to genealogists who may have ancestors who became naturalized citizens while serving in the US armed forces. With the threat of war looming on the horizon, the United States Congress passed the National Defense Act of 1916, which authorized the military to expand its ranks, and by 1917 the federal army around 121,000 servicemen, and the National Guard had a total of 181,000 servicemen.

President Wilson initially only volunteers to supply the troops needed to fight in the Great War six weeks after war was declared, only 73,000 had volunteered for service. Around 300,000 would volunteer for service before the end of the war. When America entered the Great War on April 6, 1917, Wilson authorized the military to increase its forces to one million men.

The Selective Service Act of 1917, required all males aged 21 to 30 regardless of citizenship to register for military service. Congress later amended this law in August 1918 to include all men aged 18 to 45.

As a state of war existed between the United States and her allies against the powers of Germany and the Australian Hungarian Empire, all non-naturalized citizens of those countries became enemy aliens and thus a potential threat to the American war effort.

Men and women who were non-citizens (aliens) serving in the U.S. military did not gain citizenship through service alone. The US government was intent on ensuring the allegiance of the overwhelming number of non-Americans serving in the military. This meant providing an expedient process for securing American citizenship before being shipped off to the front lines of France. Naturalization of soldiers was performed under certain provisions of nationality law facilitated by the U.S. armed forces

These provisions waived the Declaration of Intention requirement and waived or reduced the residency requirement

Naturalization of soldiers Could be performed at either:
- a Federal, State or local court having jurisdiction over the soldier's military base
- a judge from any of those courts might have held "naturalization court" at the military base

A number of soldiers filed petitions and were naturalized the same day. One copy of the petition was filed in the court where the naturalization took place, while another copy was filed with the Federal Immigration and Naturalization Service.

Look back at your research and ask yourself - what was your soldier's citizenship status?
- "Alien" – Citizen of a foreign government residing in the US
- Filed "First papers" – Submitted declaration of Intent
- Filed "Second Papers" or "Final Papers" – Submitted Naturalization Petition
- Owned a "Certificate" – Naturalization Certificate Granted
- Was Their Parent(s) naturalized?
  - All underage children would have been included in parent's application for citizenship

If you are having problems finding your ancestor's naturalization paperwork, for individuals who appeared as aliens in the 1910 census, and a naturalized citizen in the 1920 census, they may have achieved citizenship while performing military service during the Great War.

Right now, Ancestry.com is home to a database entitled *Naturalizations of World War I Soldiers*; however, it is important to note not all U.S. military bases are included on this searchable index. There is a growing number of resources available online and at the National Archives which should be able to assist you with your research.

National Archives I

Take a look the 'Alien Papers' at National Archives in Washington D.C. If you have the name of the training camp(s) where your ancestor was stationed, you may be able to find more the genealogical smoking gun of pre-immigration information available in the National Archives. By visiting the National Archives website at https://catalog.archives.gov/, use the Advanced Search option and in the Record Group use '393' & in the Keyword area fill in 'Alien Papers'. Here's a catalog shortcut for easy access. http://goo.gl/CuKkHU.

Here is a quick review of the records which provide military training camp information:
- National Personnel Records Center Official Military Personnel Files
- State and Local Discharge or Service Records and State Service Cards
- Reconstructed Service Record
- Muster Rolls (on microfilm at NPRC)
- Ancestry.com - Naturalizations of World War I Soldiers

The Alien Papers at the National Archives are the hidden gem of World War I research. Each camp kept a tally and account of individuals who were choosing to becoming naturalized, while questioning those who wished to keep their original citizenship. In addition to individual names listed (with pre and post immigration name chances), you'll also find items such as correspondence, lists of non-citizens willing or volunteering for naturalization, as well as their rank, military serial numbers, training units, and nationality.

The individual records in these collections provide a stunning amount of information on each person including:
- Name, Rank, and Unit
- Date of Birth and Entry to the United States

- Names of relatives
- Conflicts or Requests for Release from Service
- Discharge Recommendations
- Internment Recommendations

Here's one account from Camp Funston:
"Frank Batelka, Q.M.C. Detachment. Born in Horni, Kruty, Austria, December 21, 1895. Entered U.S. May 1, 1912. Home address, Stanton, Nebr. Occupation, farm laborer. Relatives uncle, James Smrkovsky, Clarkson, Nebr. Parents in Austria. Two brothers in Austrian Army. Affidavits, passport and inspection card submitted to this office in substantiation of enemy citizenship. Discharge recommended; interment deemed unnecessary."

In one short paragraph, you'll be able to find a concise summary of not only your ancestor's citizenship status, but of their birth place and date, home address, emigration date, family situation, and if any relatives are living abroad.

Military Naturalization Petitions on FamilySearch
What may surprise is the sheer number of district court military naturalization records you'll find online for free on FamilySearch (https://goo.gl/vogEdv). What throws off most researchers may be the title of these items. They are listed simply as 'Military petitions, City, State, various date – various date', and are not listed as a naturalization search result on the site. You may have seen them already and missed them completely. Now is the time to go back and take a look at these items! Locate your ancestor's military training camp location and check on the jurisdiction of each district court. If the two seem to overlap, give these records and browse online. Here are a few example titles in this collection:

- *Military Petitions, Atlanta, Georgia, 1918-1924*
- *Military Petitions, Charleston, South Carolina, 1918-1924*
- *Military Petitions, Columbia, South Carolina, 1918*
- *Military Petitions, for Birmingham, Alabama, 1918-1924*
- *Military Petitions, for Montgomery, Alabama, 1918*
- *Military Petitions, Louisville, Kentucky, 1903-1906, 1918-1921*
- *Military Petitions, Raleigh, North Carolina, 1918-1919*

- *Military Petitions, Rome Georgia, 1918*
- *Military Petitions, (Missouri) 1918*
- *Upton Military Petitions for Naturalization (New York), 1918; Index 1918-1920*
- *Michigan, Chippewa County, Naturalization records, 1918-1985*

Enemy Alien Registration and Identification Records

As non-naturalized citizens from Germany and the Austrian Hungarian Empire became enemy aliens on the day America entered World War I, the US government designed a way to keep tabs on individuals and families who posed a potential security risk to the country. In 1918, unnaturalized men and women were required to report to their local police department and fill out a form titled "United States of America, Department of Justice, Registration Affidavit of Alien Enemy". American-born women who had married an unnaturalized enemy alien also lost her US citizenship and were required to reapply for citizenship through official channels.

An enemy alien identification card complete with photograph and a fingerprint, and a card was issued to each individual when they completed their registration affidavit. These identification cards may already be part of your family's genealogical collection. What the identification card does not show you are the extensive four-page data gathering process which puts well used resources like naturalization papers or passport applications to shame.

Enemy Alien Registration Files include:
- Name of Alien & Maiden Name of Female Applicants
- Current Address Length of Residence in Community
- Birthplace and Date of Birth
- All Employment and Residences Since January 1, 1914
- Date and Port of Arrival in United States as well as the Name of the Ship
- Name of Person Who Sponsored Entry
- Names of Parents and Parents' Birthplaces
- Registrant's Marital Status and Name of spouse
- Names and Birth Dates of Children
- Whether or Not Registrant had Family Members Serving in US

Military
- Whether or Not Registrant had Family Members Serving in a Foreign Military
- Details of Individual's US/Foreign Military Service
- Naturalization Information
- Arrest Information
- Physical Description
- Photograph, Signature, and Fingerprints

Alien women were required to submit names, birth dates, and residences of all brothers and sisters, and languages spoken, written and read.

As these records were held at various police departments, courthouses, and other municipal locations, there is not one central place to search for records. Also, the federal government granted local governments the opportunity to destroy these registration files after the war.

If you're interested in this type of research, let's take a look at some examples of what records are available both online and in a physical format:

Alien Enemy Registrations, 1917 - 1920
U.S. District Court for the Eastern District of Kentucky. Frankfort Term.
National Archives at Atlanta (RE-AT)
5780 Jonesboro Road
Morrow, GA 30260
Phone: 770-968-2100
Fax: 770-968-2547
Email: atlanta.archives@nara.gov
https://catalog.archives.gov/id/5752917

Alien Registration Affidavits, 1918 - 1918 U.S. District Court for the Eastern District of North Carolina. Raleigh Term.
National Archives at Atlanta (RE-AT)
5780 Jonesboro Road
Morrow, GA 30260

Phone: (770) 968-2100
Email: atlanta.archives@nara.gov
https://catalog.archives.gov/id/5889371

Enemy Alien Registration Affidavits, 1917 - 1921 (Kansas) and *Enemy Alien Registration Affidavits, Correspondence, and Supporting Documentation, 1918 (North Dakota)*
National Archives at Kansas City (RM-KC)
400 West Pershing Road
Kansas City, MO 64108
Phone: (816) 268-8000
Email: kansascity.archives@nara.gov
Kansas - https://catalog.archives.gov/id/286181
North Dakota - https://goo.gl/85jCr7

Sample of Registration Affidavits of Alien Females in Wisconsin, 6/21/1918 - 6/26/1918
National Archives at Washington, DC - Textual Reference (RDT1)
National Archives Building
7th and Pennsylvania Avenue NW
Washington, DC 20408
Phone: (202) 357-5385
Email: Archives1reference@nara.gov
https://catalog.archives.gov/id/38983236

Case Files on Detained Enemy Aliens, 1917 - 1919
U.S. District Court for the Western (Cincinnati) Division of the Southern District of Ohio
National Archives at Chicago (RM-CH)
7358 South Pulaski Road
Chicago, IL 60629-5898
Phone: (773) 948-9001
Email: chicago.archives@nara.gov
https://catalog.archives.gov/id/17408476

Alien Registration Affidavits, 2/6/1918 - 6/28/1918
U.S. District Court for the Phoenix Division of the District of Arizona
National Archives at Riverside (RW-RS)

23123 Cajalco Rd
Perris, CA 92570
Phone: (951) 956-2000
Email: riverside.archives@nara.gov
https://catalog.archives.gov/id/294758

<u>Non-National Archive Enemy Alien Registration Files</u>
Arkansas History Commission
Affidavits for Alien Enemies in the District of Eastern Arkansas, 1918
https://goo.gl/U1gm5w

Allen County Public Library
Genealogical Records of German Families of Allen County, Indiana
https://goo.gl/Pp3fmL
Original Enemy Alien Registration Files held at Fort Wayne-Allen County Historical Society

San Francisco Public Library
Alien enemy registration affidavits, 1918. https://goo.gl/wXCFWY

Minnesota Digital Library
Alien Enemy Affidavits of Stillwater, Minnesota https://goo.gl/8NHDcN

Enemy Alien Information in FBI Files
Another place to find information on enemy aliens is by searching Fold3's collection of Federal Bureau of Investigation (FBI) Files. The FBI relied heavily on a volunteer army of private citizens called the American Protective League to gather intelligence, help investigate suspicious individuals, and send detailed reports to all the major FBI offices across the country. The APL collected a robust set of information on men and women of all ages and backgrounds. Browsing the Fold3 FBI Files online, there are four distinct record areas which may be useful in tracking your enemy alien or foreign-born ancestor.

- *Bureau Section Files, 1909-1921*
- *Mexican Files, 1909-1921*

- *Miscellaneous Files, 1909-1921*
- *Old German Files, 1909-1921*

The Old German Files on Fold3 are searchable and include details of suspicious activity (reported by members or submitted), dates of correspondence, names of investigators, name of informant, history and description of suspicious activity, resolution, action taken, and conclusion, and a copy of original documents on the case. You may have an ancestor who wasn't aware how their purchase of a large farm and the addition of a large barn may have been perceived to the APL as a potential threat to the country, as the land and barns may have been a cover for a German airplane landing strip and secret radio facility.

Enemy aliens and law-breaking US citizens alike are documented in the Fold3 FBI Files. War profiteering of commodities, Vehicle Theft (violations of the Dyer Act), Perjury, Fugitives on the run, Lottery ticket theft and Goods Trafficking are just a few of the crimes found in these files. Where these records may not precisely fulfill your World War I genealogy goals, it is an area of research which add additional information on the activities of your ancestor during this time period.

American Protective League

Records on the activities and inner workings of the American Protective League (APL) are robust, consisting of correspondence, collective reports, community talking points, membership lists, as well as oath, loyalty, and pledge documents. As the APL was organized on a local level, the name may have been changed from state to state. The APL also hosted a children's branch of the organization called the Anti-Yellow Dog League.

Some American Protective League Records can be found on Ancestry.com. This is a good place to begin your APL research:
- *Cards and Registers of Members, 1917-1919*
- *American Protective League Correspondence, 1917-1919*
- *American Protective League Newsletters, 1918*

Extensive physical APL records are available in federal, state, and university archives, as well as some historical societies.

National Archives - https://goo.gl/JbBEYu
Patriotic Societies - American Protective League
Record Group 65 - Records of the Federal Bureau of Investigation, 1896 - 2008
Record Group 165 - Records of the War Department General and Special Staffs, 1860-1952

New York City - *Patriotic Service League Records, 1917* https://goo.gl/Ut1LLW

Louisiana - *American Protective League Records 1918* https://goo.gl/jQ2v5Q

Cleveland - *The Royce Family Papers, 1852-1924* https://goo.gl/H4pq2x

Seattle - *American Protective League, Minute Men Division, Precinct 265 records, 1918-1919.* https://goo.gl/NxBNVu

Wisconsin - *Wisconsin Defense League General Correspondence, 1917-1918.* https://goo.gl/4DxN9p

Chapter 6 - Non-Military Women's World War I Records

Research into your female ancestors who may have been involved with war effort work may be easier than you realize. The role of women in the war effort was absolutely essential, and there is a rich assortment of resources documenting the activities, projects, and contributions of women during the Great War. When beginning research on your female ancestor, you will want to track down the county and city of residence during the war years, or a rough approximation of location if they lived in a relatively rural location. Examine family collections for information such as:

- Obituary Notices
- Photographs
- Old Postcards and Letters
- Personal Diaries
- Family Stories (Write what you know and record other relatives)
- Details of Membership from Social Groups and Lineage Societies
- Newspaper Clippings
- Oral Histories

Looking through these items may provide hints as to how your ancestors contributed to the war effort. Women's service extended far beyond knitting stockings and rolling bandages. Liberty loan drives, county war councils, food preservation classes, ration recipe contributions, organizing magazine and book drives, coordinating children's patriotic parades, assisting immigrant communities, and providing food and drink to soldiers at train station canteens were some of the few ways women lent their services and support.

The Women's Committee of the Council of National Defense
A majority of planned efforts undertaken by women were coordinated by the Women's Committee of the Council of National Defense. The committee was charged with coordinating the activities and resources of the organized and unorganized women of the country for the war effort.

With little more than a letter from the Secretary of Defense to guide them the committee met on May 2-5, 1917 in Washington and formulated a plan of organization and action which was approved by the Council of Defense shortly afterward. The committee coordinated with established organizations such as the Federation of Women's Clubs, the National Society of the Daughters of the American Revolution, the Colonial Dames, the United Daughters of the Confederacy, the Council of Jewish Women, the Young Women's Christian Association (YWCA), the Navy League, the Congress of Mothers, and women's union groups to provide a vast array of services and supplies for government agencies and military personnel.

While the Women's Committee coordinated with a vast array of groups and organizations, city and state councils for the committee were organized in each of the forty-eight states. At each of the state and national meetings, the committee kept a careful account of membership attendance during meetings, names from incoming and outgoing correspondence, names from submitted reports, and other information which is valued by genealogists.

While there is a small and growing collection of Women's Committee records available online, a majority of these records are available for viewing at the National Archives II in College Park. There are three great indexes to the committee's meetings available to view and download online, all three of these resources contain surnames and other genealogical data which may be useful. To access the physical records from these indexes, you'll need to visit National Archives II and request items from Record Group 62: Records of the Council of National Defense, 1916 – 1933.

***

Index to Book I of the Minutes of Meetings of the Committee on Women's Defense Work - May 2 - September 26, 1917
https://catalog.archives.gov/id/55309634

Index to Book II of the Minutes of Meetings of the Committee on Women's Defense Work -September 27 - December 19, 1917
https://catalog.archives.gov/id/55309634

Index to Book III of the Minutes of Meetings of the Committee on Women's Defense Work -January 18 - June 12, 1918
https://catalog.archives.gov/id/55309728

If you do not see your ancestor's name listed in national records, do not give up your search. State branches for the Women's Committee may be available in state or regional archives or may be included in the collections at a college or university. You may also wish to contact the society chapter or social club chapter to browse available archives or scrapbooks dating from the time period. If scrapbooks are not available from the local chapter, contact the national organization for each society.

YMCA, YWCA, & Salvation Army Records

The Young Men's Christian Association, the Young Women's Christian Association, and the Salvation Army organized an extensive series of initiatives and services which were vital for the nation's war effort. When approaching this avenue of research, use the same strategy outlined with American Red Cross records – start with local resources and work forward to state and national records access.

Family Search offers an essential record set online entitled *United States, YMCA World War I Service Cards, 1917-1919*. This collection is searchable and available for free online.

Meanwhile, a large collection of YWCA records are available on microfilm at Smith College, with a description of the records available at https://asteria.fivecolleges.edu/findaids/sophiasmith/mnsss292.html.

The Salvation Army National Archives and Research Center is home to an extensive collection of books, archival documents, microfilm, and periodicals. This archive requests research appointments in advance to ensure staff will be available for in-person assistance. Contact information and other details are available online: https://www.loc.gov/rr/main/religion/sa.html.

Labor and Trade Union Records

There was a real social divide between working class women and those of an elevated socioeconomic income. In the shifting landscape of wartime America, some of these social distinctions were beginning to level out, especially as women of all income levels were banding together to contribute to the war effort, as well as the women's suffrage movement. Among the list of organizers for the national Women's Committee was American labor leader Agnes Nestor, who served as a leader of both the International Glove Workers Union (IGWU) and the Women's Trade Union League (WTUL).

Manufacturing and factory labor undertaken by women were essential to the creation of war materials both before and during America's participation in World War I. This contribution was documented in thoroughly in a report entitled *The New Position of Women in American Industry* (https://goo.gl/LB1ZuY) published in 1920 by the US Department of Labor.

Women's union and trade records, especially those for large urban centers, provide an avenue of research for female ancestors who may not have had the time or social collateral to join a lineage society or volunteer organization. Depending on your ancestor's location, there are resources available at state archives, historical societies, and in the national archives system to help you with this area of research.

Here are a few examples:

Women's Trade Union League of Chicago collection, 1908-1944 at the University of Illinois at Chicago Library - https://goo.gl/Wj3eh7

Papers of the Women's Trade Union League and its Principal Leaders,

1855-1964 on Microfilm - https://goo.gl/SqgTg2

National Women's Trade Union League of America on Microfilm - https://goo.gl/AL6C7X

Glove Workers' Journal, published by the International Glove Workers Union of America is available at the Chicago History Museum and the Wisconsin Historical Society - https://goo.gl/kN6aDC

Online Books – The Treasure Trove of Women's Information

Unlike previous generations, a number of ladies who contributed to the war effort were quick to document and publish books highlighting the projects and activities undertaken by women on a local, regional, and national level. These some of these publications are being digitized and made available online for free, but it is important to research what resources are available in a non-digital format from a historical and genealogical societies, as well as items which may be located in local, state, or regional libraries and archives. Here are a few recommended titles containing genealogical data on female ancestors of the World War I era.

American Women and the World War by Ida Clyde Clarke on Hathi Trust https://goo.gl/Ug1MCk

Davidson County (Tennessee) Women in the World War, 1914-1919 by Rose Long Gilmore on ExLibris https://goo.gl/AbkNKx

Contributions of individual women and women's organizations are often documented in the county honor roll and county history books published just after the war. These books may have a variety of titles and publishers, and your ancestor's county may have more than one of these types of books available.

For example the *Honor Roll and Complete War History of Genesee County, Michigan, in the Great World War 1914 to 1918* on Internet Archive (https://goo.gl/tgiuCC) contains the following information on Red Cross volunteers, nurses, and additional female non-combatants:

- City Division of the Women's Organization Genesee County War Board (Names and photographs)
- Township Chairmen of the Women's Organization Genesee County War Board (Names and photographs)
- Army School of Nursing Graduates (names only)
- Genesee County Women Who Served in the Great War (Names, details, and photographs)
- Army Nurses (Names, details, and photographs)
- Officers of the Genesee Chapter of the American Red Cross, as well the names of volunteers in the county
- Detailed Descriptions of Red Cross Events, Committee Projects, and Community Impact.
- YMCA and Knights of Columbus Members Serving in the Military (Names, Photographs, and Service Details)
- Junior Red Cross Highlights and Names of Members
- Liberty Loan Funding Drives and Projects

Some of the county history books of World War I include and are not limited to the following:
- *Martin County in the World War, 1917-1919*
- *Waseca County, Minnesota in the World War*
- *Hancock County, Indiana, in the World War, 1914-1918*
- *Ripley County's part in the World War, 1917-1918*
- *Andover, Massachusetts, in the World War*
- *The University of Maine and the War*
- *Penn State in the World War*

With the project details and other events chronicled in honor roll and county histories war books, check for additional articles published in the local newspaper. It was the responsibility of each committee to keep their own correspondence, scrap book items, and other memorabilia on their own.

You may also wish to contact your local state or local archive for Red Cross scrap books which were compiled during the Great War. These may still be held privately by individuals or in a public access depository. Here are a few examples of county Red Cross chapter records available for researchers:

Red Cross Records

The difficult distinction you may be struggling with is finding supporting documentation linking a female ancestor with the American Red Cross as a volunteer or serving as a trained Red Cross nurse. Through a collection of records available online and in physical formats, you may find a relative who served as a volunteer, a nurse, or both.

To locate an ancestor's volunteerism with the Red Cross, you will want to start on a local level for county or city chapter records and published accounts written shortly after the Great War. Depending on the publication, county histories of World War I cited previously may contain war effort contributions made by groups and organizations throughout the county including Red Cross volunteers and nurses. In addition to the World War I honor rolls and county histories, individual Red Cross chapters wrote, compiled, or published the names of their volunteers as well as an account of their war work between 1919 and the mid-1920s.

The North Carolina State Archives hosts an amazing array of over sixty compiled county Red Cross chapter histories for the state (https://goo.gl/2pu8WA), most of which are online and available for free to browse and research. State archives Military Collection Archivist Matthew M. Peek published an interesting blog post about this collection, which provides research information on World War I era Red Cross records across the state and provides highlights from the collection as well. You can read more about it here: https://www.ncdcr.gov/blog/2017/11/28/history-north-carolina-red-cross-wwi-chapter-histories

There is a wide array of county, city, and state Red Cross histories online such as:
- *A Red Cross Chapter at Work* (Indianapolis, IN) by Marie Cecile and Anselm Chomel available on Hathi Trust - https://babel.hathitrust.org/cgi/pt?id=wu.89088272182;view=1up;seq=12
- *American Red Cross District of Columbia Chapter Report of War Relief Activities 1917-1919* available online at Internet Archive

https://archive.org/stream/reportofwarrelie00redc#page/n3/mode/2up
- *History Of Detroit Chapter, American Red Cross, Detroit, Michigan to June 31, 1919* available online from the University of Michigan - https://goo.gl/nqJ6fo
- *The Pittsburgh Chapter, American Red Cross; a History of the Activities of the Chapter from its Organization to January 1, 1921, with an Appendix Containing All Available Names of Those Who Rendered Red Cross Service During that Period* available online from Hathi Trust https://catalog.hathitrust.org/Record/008643514

You can cross-reference the activities, projects, and duties undertaken at the local level with what is chronicled in the Red Cross Bulletin, one of the official publications published by the American Red Cross during World War I. This series is available for free to download and research online at Hathi Trust - https://catalog.hathitrust.org/Record/008607613

Be on the lookout for online finding guides for local American Red Cross chapter records online through colleges, universities, and special archives as well as state facilities. Here are some of the more intriguing examples of what is available offline in several depositories:
- *Kansas Collection of Red Cross Chapters (Butler, Shawnee and Trego County)* available at the Kansas Historical Society - https://www.kshs.org/archives/40556
- *Records of the American National Red Cross, Northern Division (Minnesota, North and South Dakota, and Montana)* at the Minnesota Historical Society - http://www2.mnhs.org/library/findaids/01130.xml
- *Guide to the American Red Cross, Boston Metropolitan Chapter Records, 1919-1939* available at Simmons Library - https://beatleyweb.simmons.edu/collectionguides/CharitiesCollection/CC028.html
- *Indianapolis Red Cross Chapter Records* at the Indiana Historical Society - https://indianahistory.org/wp-content/uploads/american-red-cross-indpls-area-chapter-records.pdf
- *American Red Cross, Dayton Area Chapter Records* at Wright State University - https://www.libraries.wright.edu/special/

collectionguides/files/ms121.pdf
- *American National Red Cross, Washtenaw County Chapter Records: 1916-1976* available at the Bentley Historical Library - https://quod.lib.umich.edu/b/bhlead/umich-bhl-852163?view=text
- *Troup County Chapter American Red Cross Records (Georgia)* at Troup County Historical Society Archives - https://www.trouparchives.org/index.php/manuscripts/entry/troup_county_chapter

American Red Cross Nurse Files

In researching American Red Cross Nurses, there are extensive files available online through a partnership with Ancestry.com and the National Archives II in College Park, Maryland. Of particular interest are the *Historical Nurse Files, ca. 1916-1959*. This series of records has recently been made available on Ancestry.com. Information on each nurse is available alphabetically by surname, which allows you to browse the collection to look at the collection as a whole. The National Archives has recently begun scanning World War I nurse application cards and photographs of individuals. These items are browsable on the National Archive catalog site. You can see more online Red Cross records from the National Archives here https://goo.gl/Ga8qTz

When making a trip to see other American Red Cross records in College Park, don't forget to dedicate a day or two in the photograph collection. Individual American Red Cross nurse photographs are available in their collection, which makes this a valuable venue for research. National Archives II also hosts an extensive photographic collection on American Red Cross groups and events held on national, state, county, and local levels. These often include group photographs which do not list surnames, however, this shortcoming would provide a great 'match the picture with the name' project for a genealogical society.

Chapter 7 - Short Guide to Researching Canadian Military World War I Records

If one country deserves an award for best of show for World War I records, it's Canada. In contrast to the challenge posed by research in the United States, a multi-year effort to make Canadian records readily available to researchers online well ahead of the centennial. Researching veterans of the Great War in Canada is a straight forward exercise, which is a tremendous advantage to genealogists of all skill levels. Researchers with American ancestors who enlisted in the Canadian military should use the following guidelines to collect information.

Library and Archives Canada contains the following items for free in a downloadable files:
- Attestation Papers
- Military Service Records
- Unit War Diaries
- Imperial War Service Gratuity Files

Library and Archives Canada has spent several years digitizing their enlistment and military service records and making them available online for free. Attestation papers were the first step in the enlistment process, providing personal details such as date of birth, birth place, skills, physical features, address, and next of kin information. These files are two to three pages and are filled in by the individual at the time of enlistment.

Library and Archives Canada has completed their digitization of these records. They are available on their website at https://www.bac-lac.gc.ca/eng/discover/military-heritage/first-world-war/personnel-records/Pages/search.aspx. Each veteran in the database will have their attestation information and military service file available on the same page.

The military service files kept by Canada during the Great War include a treasure trove of information, from enlistment and training data, to hospital admission and treatment information, metals received during service, and dental records.

It may be a temptation to overlook or skip the Great War Unit Diaries available at the Library and Archives Canada. The website housing items in this record have a disclaimer on the lack of personal details naming individual soldiers in each unit. While these entries are less of a 'dear diary' and more of a Facebook check-in on a specific geographical location, there are mentions of individuals entering or departing the unit on leave, as well as accounts of staff transfers. As these are geographical and daily accounts of the actions of the unit, autopsy and disciplinary actions are sometimes referenced in these records.

Additional Records Online

There has been a wave of resources added to major genealogical websites within the last several years. As Canada was part of the British Empire at the time of the Great War, several of the country's record sets will sometimes be placed in the list of records belonging that collection. Without going through some of the philosophical and historical reasons why this 'double check' of records exists, just accept that the system of collecting and filing paperwork from a century ago does not necessarily coincide with how genealogists access records in today's digital age.

With that in mind, here is a short list of Canadian World War I records which are available through several sites:

Ancestry
- *Canada, Soldiers of the First World War, 1914-1918*
- *Canada, Military Honours and Awards Citation Cards, 1900-1961*
- *Canada, Nominal Rolls and Paylists for the Volunteer Militia,*

1857-1922
- *Canada, War Graves Registers (Circumstances of Casualty), 1914-1948*
- *Canada, CEF Commonwealth War Graves Registers, 1914-1919*
- *Canada, Militia and Defence Forces Lists, 1832, 1863-1939*
- *Canada, Certificates of Military Instruction, 1867-1932*
- *U.S., Residents Serving in Canadian Expeditionary Forces, 1917-1918*

Fold3
- *WWI Canadian Soldiers*
- *Airmen Died in the Great War*
- *British Army Recipients of the Military Medal*
- *British Army WWI Pension Records*
- *British WWI Service Women Casualties*
- *Canada, Ledgers Of CEF Officers Transferring To Royal Flying Corps*
- *Queen's Canadian Military Hospital Registers*
- *UK, Army Registers Of Soldiers' Effects*
- *UK, Courts Martial Registers*
- *UK, Military Deserters*
- *UK, Royal Air Force Airmen Records, 1918-1940*

Planning an On-Site Visit

Library and Archives Canada
395 Wellington St
Ottawa, ON K1A 0N4
http://www.bac-lac.gc.ca/eng/Pages/home.aspx
Phone: (613) 996-5115

As the act of gathering Canadian Great War military service records is a rather straightforward process, it is easy to overlook the wealth of additional information housed at the Library and Archives of Canada. Military service files are just the first step of research gathering, so it is important to pair service files with other resources online such as:

- Unit War Diaries of the First World War
- Courts-Martials of the First World War
- Military Medals, Honours and Awards, 1812–1969
- Personnel Records of the First World War
- Service Files of the Royal Canadian Navy, 1910-1941 - Ledger Sheets
- Circumstances of Death Registers, First World War
- Commonwealth War Graves Registers, First World War
- Veterans Death Cards: First World War

To request physical items from the collection, make sure your requests for items pertaining to your research are submitted using the guidelines listed online at http://www.bac-lac.gc.ca/eng/services-public/Pages/services-public.aspx#b. Use the finding aids, online research help, and e-mail inquiries well in advance of your visit. Allow for extra time to register and receive a user card to access the collection. This will ensure you will have the best possible experience going through materials. If you are planning to use your own camera to photograph records, check with staff regarding the use of tripods and flash photography beforehand. You may wish to purchase your own equipment in advance or checkout available items on site.

Canadian War Museum
1 Vimy Place
Ottawa, ON K1A 0M8
https://www.warmuseum.ca
P 1-800-555-5621

When you're finished gathering materials at the Library and Archives of Canada, set aside an additional day or two to visit and conduct research at the Canadian War Museum. The museum complex is about a

15 minute walk from Library and Archives Canada. Visit the museum, it's excellent! When you are ready to return to your research, visit the museum's Military History Research Centre, which offers an outstanding collection of materials and resources to fill in the gaps in your research. Use the online cataloge to browse materials at https://goo.gl/jNqFLW. While the research centre is open to the general public, it is advisable to schedule an appointment in advance for personalized assistance and research on specific people and military units.

FOL
NOV 1 0 2024

10530752R00052

Made in the USA
Lexington, KY
24 September 2018